About the Author

J. Williamson received her B.A. in biology and environmental education at Gettysburg College, and writes a monthly newsletter for naturalists and teachers published by the Pennsylvania Bureau of State Parks. Denise is editor and author of a major work, *A Handbook for Environmental Educators and Interpreters*, published by the state of Pennsylvania. In addition, she has written more than 40 pamphlets on themes related to nature, culture, and history. Numerous articles written by Denise have been published in Christian periodicals.

Denise lives with her husband Gary, a minister of the Mennonite Church, and her two sons, Joel and Joshua, in Birdsboro, Pennsylvania.

BIBLE READINGS SERIES

Bible Readings for Women
  Lyn Klug

Bible Readings for Men
  Steve Swanson

Bible Readings for Parents
  Ron and Lyn Klug

Bible Readings for Couples
  Margaret and Erling Wold

Bible Readings for Singles
  Ruth Stenerson

Bible Readings for Families
  Mildred and Luverne Tengbom

Bible Readings for Teenagers
  Charles S. Mueller

Bible Readings for Mothers
  Mildred Tengbom

Bible Readings for Teachers
  Ruth Stenerson

Bible Readings for Students
  Ruth Stenerson

Bible Readings for the Retired
  Leslie F. Brandt

Bible Readings for Church Workers
  Harry N. Huxhold

Bible Readings for Office Workers
  Lou Ann Good

Bible Readings for Growing Christians
  Kevin E. Ruffcorn

Bible Readings for Caregivers
  Betty Groth Syverson

Bible Readings for Troubled Times
  Leslie F. Brandt

Bible Readings for Farm Living
  Frederick Baltz

Bible Readings on Prayer
  Ron Klug

Bible Readings on Hope
  Roger C. Palms

Bible Readings on God's Creation
  Denise J. Williamson

Bible Readings

ON GOD'S CREATION

Bible Readings

ON GOD'S CREATION

•

Denise J. Williamson

AUGSBURG Publishing House • Minneapolis

BIBLE READINGS ON GOD'S CREATION

Copyright © 1987 Augsburg Publishing House

Library of Congress Cataloging-in-Publication Data

Williamson, Denise J., 1954-
    Bible readings on God's creation / Denise J. Williamson.
      p. cm.—(Bible readings series)
    ISBN 0-8066-2277-6
    1. Creation—Meditations.   I. Title.   II. Series.
    BS652.W53   1987   87-15326
    231.7'65—dc19   CIP

Manufactured in the U.S.A.   APH 10-0696

1 2 3 4 5 6 7 8 9 0 1 2 3 4 5 6 7 8 9

*To Gary, my husband,
and to our parents—
Mark and Arlene Lipper
(who gave me a love for both nature
and writing)
and
Roger and Janet Williamson
(who helped build our house
by the lake).*

PREFACE

The famous 19th-century naturalist Louis Agassiz once wrote, ". . . my experience in prolonged scientific investigations convinces me that a belief in God—a God who is behind and within the chaos of vanishing points of human knowledge—adds a wonderful stimulus to those who attempt to penetrate into the regions of the unknown."

This book has been written in the belief that awe for God and interest in nature complement one another. The devotions deal with those things that can easily be seen and tried for yourself. For this reason, it can be a sourcebook for camp counselors, teachers and retreat planners who wish to conduct outdoor worship services or organize reflective "worship walks" on one particular theme.

My greatest hope, however, is that you will take your Bible and devotional guide outdoors for personal times of meditation. I pray that from these 100 reflections you will learn more about the "Author of Life" by perusing his works. As you do, I believe, you will be sowing seed for new sources of appreciation, for the wind in our face is like that which actually brushed Jesus' cheek and the soil at our feet contains particles of ancient bedrock from God's own design. *Go forth in joy!*

■ STANDING IN BETWEEN

Ps. 103:8-12: ". . . as far as the east is from the west, so far has he removed our transgressions from us" (v. 12).

Sunrise brings an interesting play of lights to the landscape as well as to the sky. At dawn, objects between you and the eastern horizon appear as black silhouettes. On the other hand, objects beside and behind you are bathed in soft light. The refraction of light makes the eastern sky and the morning clouds full palettes of pastel colors. In contrast, the western sky is still draped with darkness.

The morning sky gives us a beautiful picture of the believer's relationship with God. Because of the Creator's grace and forgiveness, we have the opportunity to dwell in the light of his presence. "Those who look to him are radiant . . .," says Ps. 34:5. Yet, there are times when we choose sin over righteousness. Then, wrong attitudes and acts stand as black barriers between us and the perfect source of light. Continually, we must check to make sure that nothing stands between ourselves and God. Only then can God shed light onto every facet of our lives. Only then can each sin that darkened our way be hurled behind us into the blackness.

 As I meditate on my life-style, Lord, I see these barriers standing between you and me: (confess each sin that comes to mind). Thank you, Lord, for forgiving me.

Make a photographic record of the effects of sunrise on a particular landscape.

11

■ GROWING IN THE LIGHT

Eph. 5:8-10:   "For the fruit of the light consists in all goodness, righteousness and truth" (v. 9).

What a difference sunlight makes! Whenever a forest is removed because of lumbering, development or fire, sun-loving seedlings thrive. At first, disturbed areas are bare and marred with debris. Quickly, though, this unloveliness is covered by adventuresome grasses and flowering weeds. In time, shrubs and even trees add to the diversity. The trend toward predictable stages of plant growth is called *succession*. It is an important dynamic of every plant community.

Succession takes place in a spiritual sense, too. When we accept Christ as Savior, his light illuminates our life. Many of our sinful habits perish in the floodlight of purity that spurs us to repentance. Our growth after that consists of a slow clearcutting process which continually bares the base motivations that nurture our shortcomings. It is a painful process at times, but we take courage as we see the "fruit of the light" starting to form. Watch for examples of spiritual succession in the Scriptures and in your daily life.

 Almighty God, you are the true light. Free me from the darkness of my former self in order that I may bear more fruit for your glory.

Explore a field. Look for tree stumps, cornstalks, construction debris or any other clues to the area's former nature.

■ KNOWING WHAT IS TO COME

Isa. 42:1-9: ". . . before they spring into being I announce them to you" (v. 9).

Various plants and animals get ready for spring even before we're convinced that the seasons are changing. Birds begin singing their summer songs while snow still is on the ground. Tree buds expand when nights still have below-freezing temperatures. Waterfowl are restless for migration while the land still is gripped by icy weather. Studies show that many plants and animals have internal "biological clocks" whose workings often are triggered by changes in the length of nights and days. This innate ability to "tell time" allows nature, in a sense, to be ready for what is to come.

God's written Word provides us with a kind of "spiritual clock" that allows us to know, to a large degree, what the future holds for the human race. Even though we do not have specific dates for the fulfillment of God's plan, we know that Christ's return and God's final judgment are imminent. We are certain of what lies ahead because of the integrity of God's Word which has proved itself to be truth throughout history. It is for us to adhere faithfully to God's Word and to be prepared for what we know will come to pass.

 Lord, help me to live each day with the anticipation of your future glory in the new kingdom which will come into being at the end of time.

Watch the activities of animals and plants in your neighborhood and see what preparations are being made for the coming season.

■ FINDING THE WAY OUT

1 Cor. 10:1-13: ". . . he will also provide a way out. . ." (v. 13).

If several seeds are planted under a box, the seedlings will probably perish because of the lack of light. If, however, even one hole for sunlight is provided in that box, one or more seedlings may be able to make their way toward the source of light and eventually grow out through that hole. A plant's ability to bend away from the darkness and toward the light is based on a hormonal response that causes stem cells on the dark side to lengthen more rapidly than stem cells in the light.

The principle of *phototropism* is interesting to consider, especially when we face temptation in our daily lives. The Old Testament gives us clear warnings that death is the result of staying with the dark things that God does not condone. The New Testament gives us courage to resist temptation because of its promise that God will not let us be tested beyond our ability to resist. The plant world gives us a living image of what the nature of our victory over temptation will be by showing us what it looks like to turn away from darkness and grow toward the light.

 Dear God, help my consistent response to be a turning away from darkness and a growing toward light.

In a forest, study the interesting growth arrangements of plants caused by phototropism.

■ BEAUTY TO BE SEEN

Matt. 6:22-23: "If your eyes are good, your whole body will be full of light" (v. 22).

Many in our daily routine are out to manipulate our seeing. Billboard artists know what draws our attention, layout experts know which part of the newspaper page we will read first, advertising companies know how to create subconscious associations between their products and appealing settings. All of them try to capture our eye so that they can convince our mind of the messages that have priority for them.

Nature, on the other hand, does no such thing. Even though a splendid waterfall or a glamorous autumnal mountain peak may occasionally dazzle us, for the most part, nature's beauties must be sought out by the observer. Because we are so used to being manipulated, most of us need practice at really *seeing* nature's intricate and extraordinary details. One way to get this practice is to take a half-hour walk and go only *ten* feet! This type of "miniwalk" may, at first, seem absurd. But, as you look for things to make the time pass, you will begin to realize that there is much more along the trail than first meets the eye. You'll find that even the smallest pebbles, petals and puddles are wonders to behold. Miniwalks can become a source of rest and relaxation as well as a fitness exercise for the eye.

 Slow me down, Lord, and let me savor each miracle of life.

Take "miniwalks" this week in at least three different locations.

■ THE FRAGRANCE OF CHRIST

2 Cor. 2:14-17: "For we are to God the aroma of Christ. . ." (v. 15).

Fragrances affect our lives in subtle ways. Fumes from a bakery, for example, may cause us to ignore our diets. A favorite cologne might boost our self-esteem. Smells can also trigger flashbacks. Woodsmoke takes us back to a traumatic fire. Then, too, fragrances are directly responsible for the ants in our pantries (because these insects rely partially on chemical scent trails for direction), for the moth damage to our trees (because females in many species obtain mates by emitting attractants), and for the honey on our tables (because bees can recognize others from their group by odor).

Studies show that in some cases animals can detect individual molecules of certain substances. Certain chemicals aid fish in navigation, insect parasites in finding hosts, and dogs in following the master's trail. Some chemicals that are emitted by insects can either attract or repel depending on the conditions under which they are given off and received.

Such scientific information deepens our appreciation for the phrase that describes Christians as the "aroma of Christ." Certainly, inherent in the comparison is the idea that the church should be emitting a subtle, consistent, almost indefinable at times, stimulus that causes those in the world to increase their hungering after God.

 Lord, let my life be a fragrant offering to you today.

Disrupt an ant trail by laying a piece of paper across the path. Watch as the ants reestablish the trail.

■ FLESH AND BLOOD

Ps. 115:1-8: "Our God is in heaven" (v. 3).

One of the incredible things about the Creator is that he presented himself to us in flesh and blood with senses like our own. Our personal relationship with Jesus makes the psalmist's description of false gods particularly bleak. "Who," we ask, "would be foolish enough to trust such things?" But wait—don't riches, "sound" investments and many other *things,* all totally unsensing, fit the role of false gods in our day?

Spending time with nature, away from our manufactured environment, can lessen the hold that material things have on us. Outdoors, we can develop an appreciation for wild things. We can smell the pines, feel the breeze, hear the brook and know that our God relates to these experiences because as Christ he had sensory experiences like our own. What's more, he is the living God of heaven who shares our pleasure in creation, for it is the work of his hands, even as we are.

 God, thank you that you are my all-knowing friend. Thank you for enhancing my life with the gifts of senses. Let my use of them always be pleasing to you.

Use four of your five senses—seeing, hearing, smelling and touching—to explore a wild area near your home.

■ LEARNING TO LISTEN

Matt. 13:10-17: ". . . though hearing, they do not hear or understand" (v. 13).

Christ's spoken words held no wisdom for the many listeners who had no desire to truly know God. Those who did understand and did accept Christ's message were the ones whose hearts and lives began to change to match their Maker's.

In nature, there are many sounds. All remain meaningless to those who have no desire to understand them. Yet, with effort, you can train yourself to know the call of every familiar bird in your region or the source of every insect song that makes its way through your window on the night breezes. Records and tapes are readily available as aids to learning how to interpret the sounds you hear in nature. Actually *learning* to recognize the many voices of outdoor creatures, however, takes much work and persistence.

So does recognizing God's voice and knowing God's will. Commitment to Christ in a salvation experience is only the start of our need to discern God's voice from all others. We must commit ourselves to the regular study of his word. We must constantly be practicing our listening skills with him. Only then will we be able to conform routinely to his will. The reward of our ardent endeavors will be a more intimate relationship with God and a greater insight into areas of living that remain mysterious to unbelievers.

 God, help me to understand your written words and to hear your voice.

With the aid of a record or tape, learn the songs of three common birds.

18

■ BEING SILENT

Job 12:7—13:13: "But ask the animals, and they will teach you" (v. 12:7).

Job's well-spoken defense makes at least two of his beliefs clear. First, of all created beings, human beings are the only ones who challenge God. Birds and fish do not conjure up alternatives to the truth or elaborate on arguments against God's plans. Reptiles and mammals do not question the statement that "In his hand is the life of every created being, and the breath of all mankind" (v. 10).

Second, God alone has eternal power and authority. Only God has the ability to build and to destroy, to restrain and to bless, to defend and to devour. God's multiplicity of action is a sign of his ability to accomplish his perfect will.

The science-based foundation that supports our modern thinking does much to deemphasize God's role in nature. In this century, we pride ourselves in our ability to link cause and effect and to explain the working of each natural phenomenon by our understanding of chemistry, physics and other sciences. To a large degree, God has blessed our mental efforts and has given us even more proof of God's remarkable design for nature. Yet, often our haughty approach to study crowds out our reverence and our awe. It is then that we would be wise to listen to Job's firm rebuke: "If only you would be altogether silent! For you, that would be wisdom" (13:5).

 Lord, let me never be so impressed with my own thinking that I forget your words.

Today, spend a half hour outdoors in silence before God.

■ A NAME FOR EACH

Gen. 2:15-20: "He brought them to the man to see what he would name them" (v. 19).

The man's recorded name is "Adam," the Hebrew word for "man." He was the first of all created beings to have a name. God himself brought each animal in its turn before the man, and God allowed Adam to choose the name for each animal. The biblical account gives no clues as to what kinds of animals Adam saw, nor does it give us a record of the creatures' names. The event does reflect God's plan to give man preeminence over all other creatures. And, perhaps, in no other place in the Bible is there a more beautiful example of God's and man's working together in the perfect kingdom that existed before the fall.

The naming of creatures has continued, probably almost nonstop, since Adam's day. In its simplest form, fathers and mothers pass on the knowledge of common names to their children. In its most complex state, zoologists convene regularly at an international congress to hash out the names for newly discovered or reclassified organisms. Their task is overwhelming, for there are over a million known animal species. Much diversity in opinion exists on how these animals should be named and classified. Latinized scientific names that are accepted worldwide among zoologists are essential for communications and study. The process of selecting names, however, is entirely different than that tranquil task that man and God accomplished in celebration of life on the newly formed earth.

 God, thank you that you know me by name.

Trace the origin of a common animal's name.

■ A GOD-GIVEN ADDRESS

Psalm 16: "The boundary lines have fallen for me in pleasant places" (v. 6).

Each plant and animal in nature has its habitat, its physical place to live. The boundaries of one habitat may be extremely limited. Forest insects, for example, often live in only one part of one certain species of tree. Other animals dwell only in one level of the forest. Certain warblers live only high in the trees, while other birds, such as the wood thrush, dwell only in the low branches of the undergrowth.

Temperature, soil type, moisture and sunlight are some of the determinants of plant habitats. Animal habitats depend on specific associations with living things as well as physical factors. Each forest, field, lake, etc., is a community populated by individuals living at various "addresses." An experienced naturalist can predict the presence of specific animals and plants just by knowing the habitats present. The use of unique living spaces is one of nature's means to harmony.

Psalm 16 reminds us that we, as Christians, have a habitat also. It is designated and defined by God. It is in close proximity to himself. Only there will we find safety, joy and eternal harmony. Each day we should make sure that we are dwelling in the place God has designated for us. To be found anywhere else, in God's eyes, is to be living at the "wrong address."

 God, help me to know and live within the boundaries that you have set for me. Give me wisdom to see the pleasures and purposes that my unique dwelling place holds.

Read about and then observe for yourself the habitats of at least three wild creatures.

■ BUSY, YET STILL

Isa. 32:14-18: "The fruit of righteousness will be peace" (v. 17).

Most would say that *quietness* is one of the benefits of taking a walk through a summer field. But if you listen closely, summer fields really aren't very quiet. There is the constant underlying hum of innumerable insects and other creatures busy with daily tasks. What, then, is the sense of quietness that we perceive amid this incessant busyness?

Perhaps we sense tranquility in the field because each organism is accomplishing its search for food, moisture and shelter without worry. There is no striving to outdo the life-style of any other species. Each creature does what it was created to do, and a certain harmony reigns over all.

We should be looking for a similar mixture of busyness and harmony in our own lives. Unlike non-Christians, we need not be filled with the tensions of trying to prove our worth to ourselves and to others. Our self-identity and value already have been established by our relationship to God who redeemed us by his Son. Moment by moment, we can trust the same promise that comforted Moses as he led the people of Israel: "My presence will go with you, and I will give you rest" (Exod. 33:14). Our quietness will come by trusting God; our busyness will be the work of daily following God's directions for us.

 God, replace this worry (*name specific items*) and this impulse to hurry with your own peace and rest.

Take a leisurely walk and listen to the sounds of a field.

■ THE WATER OF LIFE

John 4:4-15: "Sir, give me this water so that I won't get thirsty" (v. 15).

Thirst. In the hot, dry environs of the New Testament, it was a constant, nagging demand. Even prior to Jesus' discussion with the Samaritan woman, Jews spoke in terms of the human thirsting for spiritual (or living) "water." Our modern understanding of the body's need for water only amplifies the ancient comparison.

Internal water is necessary in every organism for the transportation of nutrients and the removal of wastes. Environmental conditions often make water hard to obtain. In the desert, cacti conserve the limited resource with their needlelike leaves; animals do it with their nighttime life-styles. Special internal adaptations help the Arabian camel to go without water for as long as three months. The desert's kangaroo rat can even use the water molecules released by the internal breakdown of its food.

The thirsting soul is a different matter. God provides only one source that satisfies and one means to that source. The only living water for our spiritual thirst is Jesus Christ.

 Let my physical thirst, Lord, remind me of my urgent spiritual need to continuously be nourished and cleansed by Christ.

Set up a water source for your backyard wildlife and observe the activity around it.

■ PURE WATERS

Ps. 104:5-18: "He makes springs pour water into the ravines; it flows between the mountains" (v. 10).

Psalm 104 gives a beautiful, poetic summary of the water cycle on which all life depends. Rains and springs join to make streams. Rivers grow and find their way to the seas. Before they do, however, their waters are taken out and returned again and again to support human communities along the way.

To be pure naturally, waters must collect in a clean watershed (that portion of land that gives up its surface water to one stream or lake or reservoir). With pollution at every turn, today's domestic water sources often must be treated chemically to make them safe for use.

Mind and heart pollutants are rampant in our society as well, and there are no chemical treatments to negate their effects. The mature Christian works to focus only on things that are noble, right, pure, lovely, admirable, excellent or praiseworthy (see Phil. 4:8), for the psalmist's words still hold true: "How can a young man keep his way pure? By living according to your word" (Ps. 119:9).

 Help me today, Lord, to set my mind and heart on things that are right in your eyes.

Hike through a well-preserved, clean watershed and let its beauty meet your mental and spiritual needs.

■ SONGS FROM THE HEART

Ps. 104:31-34: "I will sing to the Lord all my life" (v. 33).

Some nature lovers are disillusioned by the fact that birds do not necessarily sing because they're *happy.* Actually, the birds' songs serve two purposes. With them, males attract mates, and territorial boundaries are established and maintained among birds of the same species. For these reasons, the spring woods and fields overflow with music.

The lovely choruses, in one sense, are nothing more than the result of chemical activities triggered in the birds' brains by the longer length of days. Even so, scientific explanations cannot distract from the beauty of a bird song.

Knowing more about the communication patterns of the birds can give us insight into the nature of praise. Too often we think that happiness must be the justification for our singing. Perhaps you don't sing at church or in your home when you don't feel happy. Yet the Scriptures command us to make praise a daily offering to God.

So, sing to the Lord each day, apart from your feelings. The outcome may surprise you. Just as the bird songs cheer us though they have little or nothing to do with happiness, so, too, you may find daily singing to cause rejoicing both in your heart and in the heart of God.

 Lord, today I sing your praise with the following song. (Choose a chorus or hymn and sing it to God.)

Keep a hymnal handy this week, and commit one of your favorite hymns to memory.

■ WEATHER REPORTS

Ps. 147:7-20: ". . . he stirs up his breezes, and the waters flow" (v. 18).

Unless there is a pending drought, the local weather report usually calls rain, snow, and other forms of precipitation "bad weather." This reflects our natural reluctance to welcome any weather that does not fit in with our day's plans. Yet, precipitation is essential to life itself. For this reason we should make it a practice to thank God for each day's weather, whether it is good or bad.

Matthew 5:45 tells us that both the righteous and the unrighteous experience the same weather. Only believers, however, have the opportunity to trust that God is in control of the weather that comes. The resulting peace that this trust gives is unattainable for those who do not accept God's sovereignty. Our daily gratefulness, regardless of the weather report, may be just what is needed to start a conversation about our Lord with someone who has no faith. Our ability to take each day's weather as a gift from God may also help us when storms invade other aspects of our life. In the same pattern as physical weather, dark clouds of pain and sadness can overtake us for a time. On those days we must ask God's help in seeing these trials as a watering of our souls. God can sustain us as we accept each of these dark days. We are not like unbelievers. Their only recourse in similar circumstances is to dwell on foiled plans and dampened dreams.

 God, thank you that I do not have to fear "bad-weather reports" in my life. I trust that you are caring daily for my needs.

Say only positive things about the weather this week.

■ UNDER GOD'S CULTIVATION

Ps. 65:9-13: ". . . the hills are clothed with gladness" (v. 12).

The psalmist paints a picture of peace and productivity by capturing the beauty of farmland. Even though today's agricultural practices differ greatly from those of the psalmist's time, we can relate to his descriptions.

Seldom do we think about the severe changes that had to take place to bring the land under cultivation. Ancient timbers were destroyed. Wildlife was driven away. For its new masters, the wilderness gave up every trait of its former nature. In return, unfortunately, "tamed" lands often showed evidences of abuse rather than of wise use. Yet, under the direction of a concerned and caring farmer, agricultural acres become living examples of productivity and peace.

Unlike the land, we have the opportunity to choose our masters. If we live life "wildly" and try to be our own boss, evidences of life abuse rather than of life's fruitful use encroach upon us. On the other hand, if we submit ourselves to the discipline and direction of God's all-knowing Shepherd, we find ourselves thriving under his perfect care. Then our thoughts dwell not on what we have given up for Christ, but on what tremendous blessings we have gained.

 God, help me to be all that you want me to be.

Take a walk or a leisurely drive through farmland and imagine Christ beside you as your perfect shepherd.

■ CONSIDERING THE LILIES

Matt. 6:28-34: "See how the lilies of the field grow" (v. 28).

The common and localized names of many plants seem to indicate that persons in the past saw spiritual symbols in ordinary wildflowers. For this reason we have a spring, six-petaled white flower called Star-of-Bethlehem and a summer group of six-petaled wildflowers known as the false Solomon's-seals. The tall and conspicuous common mullein has earned the nicknames Jacob's staff, Peter's staff and Adam's flannel. (If you study the characteristics of the plant, you can find a justification for each one.)

Unpleasant and pesky weeds have brought down names that are associated with the devil. Devil's trumpet (jimsonweed), Devil's grip (carpetweed), Devil's vine (morning glory) and Devil's tomato (horse-nettle) can be found in most wildflower guides.

Even scientific classifications can have certain tie-ins with our faith. All of the flowers of the family *Cruciferae*, for example, display a four-petaled cross wherever they bloom. Consider the wildflowers that are common in your area and look for symbols of faith in them. Keep notes on your reflections with your wildflower field guides.

 Lord, thank you that there are flowering reminders of your beauty and faithfulness everywhere.

Read Matt. 6:28-34 aloud in the center of a flowering field.

■ MEETING EVERY NEED

Psalm 23: "I shall lack nothing" (v. 1).

We and wildlife have many things in common. Like the beasts, we need food, water, shelter and safety to survive. In nature, we see the constant struggle of the individual for survival. In our own complex and sophisticated society, however, much of the struggle for survival is masked. For many of us, food comes easily from the grocery, water flows freely from the faucet and shelter is ensured by the monthly payments to the landlord or the bank.

Since the environmental movement of the 1970s, increased emphasis has been given to humankind's place in the "web of life." Advocates of such thinking warn us that our consumption of resources and our disposal of wastes have global ramifications. In the long run, our own food, water and shelter may be threatened by selfish, shortsighted life-styles. We must be concerned about the effects we have on others in the global environment.

Of all persons, believers should be the best stewards of life's sustaining elements. We profess belief in a God whom we call the Shepherd, the provider who desires to direct us to meet our needs. Certainly, our world *would* be better if Christians were better at taking their direction from Jesus instead of from their own self-fulfilling desires.

 Lord, I confess that at times my life-style has brought injustice to others and struggles to the natural world. Help me to take my directions from you.

Visit a farm and observe how the livestock's owner meets the animals' every need.

■ ATTRACTED TO THE GOLD

Acts 2:42-47: "And the Lord added to their number daily . . ." (v. 47).

Goldenrods put a blaze of color across many a late-summer field and road clearing. The tall, bright stalks would have more admirers if the truth were known that goldenrods do not cause hayfever. That summer irritation can be attributed, in part, to the lightweight pollen of the ragweeds. The inconspicuous flowers mature about the same time as the showy golden plants. Ragweeds can afford to go unnoticed because they are effectively pollinated by the wind. On the other hand, goldenrods depend on the activity of insects for pollination.

The goldenrods' bright show is put on by hundreds of tiny flowers growing closely together. Two types of blooms—disc flowers which receive the pollen and ray flowers which have a colorful "banner" petal—grow side by side. The effectiveness of their relationship is proven by the many beetles, bees and other insects that come to feed at the stalks.

As Christians, we can see ourselves as tiny flowers of faith. Separately we are insignificant. But, as a united and stable church, we produce a golden witness that attracts outsiders.

 Almighty God, let your glory be visible to others through the witness of *(name your church)*.

Closely examine a goldenrod and look for both disc and ray flowers on the plant.

■ CLINGING SEEDS OF SIN

Col. 3:1-10: "You used to walk in these ways, in the life you once lived" (v. 7).

Beautiful blooms can entice us. But beware! Some of the most attractive flowers produce hard-to-remove hitchhiking seeds. For example, the daisylike *Bidens* (Latin for "two-toothed") have seeds with sharp prongs.

There are many other varieties of hitchhiking seeds, too. All of them rely on the effectiveness of this method of seed dispersal. When the seeds finally are removed by the animal or person who has been carrying them, they are likely to be discarded in places where they can start to grow. Learning to recognize pesky hitchhikers is the only way we can avoid association with them.

The same is true for the sins that cling so tight. We need to rely on God's word as a guidebook to making choices in life. Here we find instructions on which mannerisms to embrace and which to discard. If we learn to recognize sin, even before its seeds mature, our spiritual garments of compassion, kindness, humility, gentleness and patience will not be snagged. What's more, we will have no part in spreading evil to others.

 Lord, forgive me for the times I have walked in sinful ways and have helped sow the seeds of strife and unholiness.

Make it a practice to identify hitchhikers that you pick up on a walk by finding the plants that produced them.

■ FORGETTING THE BLOOD

Heb. 9:11-28: ". . .without the shedding of blood there is no forgiveness" (v. 22).

Of all the delicate, white wildflowers that stand tall in the fields, Queen Anne's Lace is the only one with a dark, purple bloom in the middle of the white. Wildflower guides point to this one small blossom—a drop of blood on the lace—as an identifying mark of the plant distinguishing it from all others.

In the same way, the blood of Christ should stand out as the unique and central characteristic of our Christian life. The core of our faith is that Jesus Christ died for humankind. Our appreciation of the need for blood sacrifice may be limited because of our cultural experience. In contrast, the laws and worship practices of the old covenant continually put the blood of atonement in full view of the Jewish people. To the faithful in the Old Testament, the slain goats and sheep were tangible reminders of God's purity and of their unrighteousness.

As Christians, we must remember that it was Christ's anguish and his blood that brought us back to our Creator. We must be careful not to slip into a flippant faith that emphasizes and encourages others to focus on peace, love and joy without reference to Christ's redemptive work. Otherwise, we find ourselves living out a kind of "holy humanism"—a pleasant but frail counterfeit of the solid faith.

 Father, help me to keep Christ's sacrifice on the cross as the focus of my faith and give me courage to sacrifice my life for others.

Look for Queen Anne's Lace in the fields and abandoned lots near your home.

■ WINGS OF FAITH

Acts 1:1-8: ". . . and you will be my witnesses . . ." (v. 8).

Milkweed is one of the best-known weeds, probably because of the conspicuous silky parachutes that carry its seeds far and wide in the wind. When mature, the plant's silvery gray pods crack open. Ripe, dry seeds with white tufted tops blow loose and travel long distances, causing new plants to grow where they land.

If you break open a milkweed pod before it's ripe, however, you'll see the seeds inside in a different light. Developing seeds adhere tightly together. Instead of feathery tufts, the entire clump looks like a stiff, sticky fish. Milkweed seeds never can fly until they are mature.

The first chapter of Acts gives a brief description of how the first fearful disciples gained the wings of faith necessary to spread the gospel worldwide. It took the presence of the Holy Spirit to bring the maturity needed so that they could be witnesses "to the ends of the earth." We need the Holy Spirit in the same way, today, to make us mature and to send us forth into the world.

 Lord, help me to grow to the point where I can be instrumental in a new work of faith for you.

Observe milkweed in its various stages of growth and designate some time this week for reading more on the topic of Christian maturity.

■ SIDE BY SIDE

Matt. 13:24-30: "Let both grow together until the harvest" (v. 30).

Wherever cultivated plants grow, weeds are right there competing for sunlight, moisture and soil nutrients. Any experienced farmer or gardener knows which weeds probably will trouble him in a particular setting while he is raising a certain crop. In the broadest sense, a weed is any plant that, from the human viewpoint, is growing out of place. By this definition, if a person took an interest in raising dandelions, any roses that accidentally trailed into his patch would be weeds—unwanted and unplanned-for plants. No wonder weeds are common. Aren't we always cultivating and landscaping things according to our own desires and plans?

The line between wildflower and weed is less distinct in the wild. Here we condone nature's free reign. At times we even marvel at the same plants in the wild that we work so hard to eradicate back home.

No wonder God designates no one but himself to be the final judge in the spiritual work of separating "wheat and weeds." If our perspective even in botany is so limited, how could we ever expect accuracy in judging our neighbor's quality? Until that final day of "sorting" comes, we must not take it on ourselves to destroy those who seem troublesome to us.

 God, you know the spot I have in life and the true nature of those around me. Help me to do good even toward those who make life difficult for me.

Learn the natural history of at least three weeds in your yard.

■ GROWING OUT AND TAKING IN

John 15:5-8: ". . . apart from me you can do nothing" (v. 5).

A cross-section of a tree trunk at the level of a limb is a good place to see the integration of branch and supporting stem. What begins as a small external bud with transportation tissue from the stem grows, over the years, into a strong branch that still takes nourishment through the trunk. Only because of the branch's bond with the stem, can growth and fruit occur on the branch. At its base, more and more of the branch is taken over and hidden in the ever-widening circumference of the trunk. This growing out and taking in occurs continually until the branch is removed or the tree dies.

It is little wonder that Jesus spoke of himself as the true vine. Those who heard were familiar with both the care of vineyards and the Old Testament references to Israel's being God's vine. Jesus was the fulfillment of God's word. "A shoot will come up from the stump of Jesse; from his roots a Branch will bear fruit" (Isa. 11:1). Today, consider the blessing you have in being held as closely by Jesus as the vine holds to its branch. Also, consider the importance of Christ's words that we can do nothing apart from him.

 Lord, thank you for holding me close even when my attitude is one of haughtiness and ungratefulness. Right now, I acknowledge my full dependence on you.

In pieces of firewood or in lumber, look for patterns caused by the branches of the tree.

■ MORE THAN SPARROWS

Matt. 10:28-31: ". . . not one of them falls to the ground apart from the will of your Father" (v. 29).

In the animal kingdom there is a greater chance that an organism will die than that it will live. This is why each rabbit can have as many as 25 offspring per year, for example, without causing a sudden population explosion. Under normal circumstances, some bunnies will die of disease and many others will be taken as food by other animals. Those that do mature may emigrate from their home area into adjoining territories that are vacant because of other rabbit deaths. Such population dynamics are complex and always associated with many factors including population of other organisms, habitat stability, and weather.

The same population variables that affect animals—birth, death, immigration and emigration—affect the human life. In fact, the most complex of all population dynamics deals with humankind itself. Some researchers feel that in 8000 B.C. only about 5,000,000 people lived on the face of the earth. In contrast, more than 200,000,000 were living in the United States alone by the middle of the 20th century.

Because each human being has a soul, birth, death and movement in the human population affects us greatly. Death is never easy to accept. Yet, Jesus can comfort us because he holds the beginning and the end of each created being in the palm of his tender hand.

 Jesus, help me to trust you when life is taken away.

Find out the population of your city, county, state.

■ POWERED BY FAITH

Hebrews 11: ". . . without faith it is impossible to please God" (v. 6).

Every green plant is an efficient solar-powered factory. One mature maple, for example, might make more than 3600 pounds of sugar and starch each summer. Most food production occurs in the plant's remarkably designed leaves. All totaled, these paper-thin structures (on a mature tree) may expose about a half-acre of surface area to the sun. Each leaf has an intricate vein system that supplies water and minerals taken in by the roots. Carbon dioxide, the other essential food-production ingredient, comes in through special "gate-cells" in the leaves.

Chloroplasts, cells containing chlorophyll, are the plant's machines. They give plants their green color. But, most importantly, they enable plants to use light energy as a power source. By photosynthesis, a combination of water and carbon dioxide is transformed into food and oxygen. Without chlorophyll, the intricacies of the leaf would be in vain; the sun's power would be of no use.

Faith is somewhat like the "chlorophyll" of life. We may try to emulate qualities that we admire in others, such as Moses' meekness or Samson's strength, but without faith it is impossible to make our lives really count for Christ. With faith alone comes the ability to be fed by God.

 Son of God, today let me depend totally on your light.

At dinner tonight, take stock of how each item on the menu is related to photosynthesis.

■ LET THE FLOWER FADE

1 Cor. 15:35-58: ". . . to each kind of seed he gives its own body" (v. 38).

Most wildflower field guides emphasize the beauty and variety of blooms. The seeds of wild plants, however, are just as distinct and varied. Though their beauty is subdued, the seeds' importance should not be ignored. Each is a gem capable of bringing forth new life.

Our society seems to like life in full bloom. Youth, physical beauty and excellence in achievement and vigor are rewarded. Aging and imperfection often are taken as signs of diminished importance. Those who rely on society's cues can find it difficult to accept themselves or others when the "flowers" begin to fade. Yet, both the Scriptures and the natural world give encouragement concerning what follows the blossom stage of natural life.

Physical seeds must relinquish their original form to produce plants. In the same way, Jesus said, "The hour has come for the Son of Man to be glorified. I tell you the truth, unless a kernel of wheat falls to the ground and dies, it remains only a single seed. But if it dies, it produces many seeds" (John 12:23-24). Let us take our cues from Christ and be willing to see the natural perish so that the spiritual can take root in him.

 Master Designer, you are the maker of all good things. I entrust my natural life on earth to you and look forward to what is to come.

Using a magnifying lens, study the patterns and shapes of wildflower seeds.

■ PATTERNS

Rom. 12:1-8: "... these members do not all have the same function" (v. 4).

Form and function are inseparable partners in the natural world. Each plant's and animal's physical makeup coordinates with its life-style. The thick-billed cardinal, for instance, cracks seeds to eat. The crossbills, with their distinctive beaks, are perfectly adapted for prying open pinecones. The woodcocks of the lowlands can pull their food from the mud by opening just the tips of their long bills. Everywhere you turn you can match the structure of the organism with its *niche* (mode of living).

God has designed each of us, who have accepted Christ as our Savior and Lord, to fill a certain place in the church. A refreshing freedom should be present there that allows each to contribute his or her work-offering to the good of the others. For this to happen, we must be willing to commit our total life to Christ and see what he would have us do. Being too timid to exercise our gifts or being too eager to show off our talent both are traps from the secular world. Instead, make it a point to look for God's will.

 Lord, you are the one who has suited each creature to its life-style. Suit me to the special work you have for me to do in the church.

Look through a bird field guide to familiarize yourself with physical adaptations in the avian world.

■ GROWING UP

1 Cor. 3:1-7: ". . . mere infants in Christ" (v. 1).

In nature, maturation is like clockwork. Mammals of the fields and forest nurse their babies for a specific length of time, and then the young are old enough to take on solid food. Scientists believe that the albumin content in the mother's milk is what determines how quickly offspring grow. This may be why small mammals such as guinea pigs double their weight in a few days, while human infants grow much more slowly. Plants, too, are consistent in their growth rate to the point where the description on the back of a seed packet can include the estimated number of days from germination to harvest.

God, however, does not confine our spiritual growth to such time tables. The teachings of the New Testament indicate that we have control of our spiritual maturation rate despite the fact that it is God alone who can bring about growth. For many carnal reasons, we seem to want to remain "mere men," as Paul terms it, rather than to grow up to do works of righteousness. Perhaps this is because of the discipline involved in becoming mature in Christ. According to Heb. 5:14, "solid food is for the mature, who by constant use have trained themselves to distinguish good from evil." Let us endeavor to make this a description of our own life-style.

 Lord, forgive me for falling short of your perfect will for my life. I have been lax in seeking you with my whole heart. Give me a clearer picture of your plan for me as I recommit myself to you.

Find an opportunity to watch how quickly baby animals or garden plants grow.

■ WOLF TREES

1 Thess. 2:10-12: "You are witnesses . . ." (v. 10).

Sometimes when you walk in the woods you come upon a huge tree with a crown that spreads out among the other, younger trees. Such a tree is called a "wolf tree." Often wolf trees stand as testimonies that once, perhaps decades ago, they were the only trees there. Now such elderly giants are surrounded by younger trees, some of which have sprung from their own seed. Since their far-reaching roots and branches can out-compete younger trees, modern forestry practice seldom tolerates their presence in managed areas. Still there's something special about them. Perhaps it's that they tie us to the past while freely contributing seeds that will outdo them in the future.

The church, on the other hand, can only benefit from an intergenerational testimony. We should thank God for those older than ourselves who have been conscientiously living out the faith. And as we find ourselves more and more surrounded by younger and "greener" believers, we should recognize our ministry to them. Experienced Christians testify to God's reliability. They serve as models of righteousness while sowing seeds that will ensure the continuation of faith in the next generation.

 Lord, I thank you for (name specific persons who have modeled the faith for you). I ask that you bless them with continued fruit. Help me to be a testimony and an inspiration for (name someone who is younger in faith than yourself).

Find a wolf tree near your home and spend some time meditating there.

■ COSTLY GRACE

Acts 3:11-20: "You killed the author of life, but God raised him from the dead" (v. 15).

Each year, literally *tons* of debris fall to the forest floor. Pollen grains, faded flowers, wilted leaves, broken branches and fallen trees pile up at a remarkable pace. But nature lets nothing go to waste. Insects, fungi and other organisms quickly turn this dead material into humus, the vegetative portion of soil. This humus is essential to the growth of every forest plant. Truly, in nature, life is dependent on death.

Life from death is the essence of Peter's testimony in Solomon's Colonnade as well. The "author of life" was murdered, Peter says, but God raised him from the dead. It is not by human power, Peter points out, that a lame beggar can now walk. It is by faith in Jesus that this man is well and strong.

It cost God dearly to bring wholeness to that impoverished man; the price was the blood of his own Son. It is the same costly grace that gives us the opportunity to have life instead of death, and we should never take that lightly.

 God, thank you for loving me so much that you sacrificed your Son for me. Thank you Jesus, for giving me life through your death and resurrection.

Search the forest floor for signs of decay. Find the thin line in the soil where dead plant material becomes humus.

■ ON A TREE

Acts 5:25-32: "The God of our fathers raised Jesus from the dead— whom you had killed by hanging him on a tree" (v. 30).

Our society has an insatiable demand for wood. Inks, glass, books, plastics, polishes and explosives are among the more than five thousand items derived from this natural resource. Even before technology opened the door for so many wood uses, societies understood that different trees contributed woods with different properties. Chapter 2 of 2 Chronicles preserves Solomon's message to the king of Tyre, which in part is a purchase order for the woods of cedar, pine and algum (possibly juniper). King Hiram's reply is a promise that workers will fell the logs and float them to Joppa, more than 100 miles to the south. Professional woodcutters completed the mission that supplied Solomon with the materials needed for the temple's construction.

One or more woodcutters also were responsible for providing the crucifixion crosses used in Jerusalem. Certainly it would have been beyond their imaginations to believe that one day God himself would die upon one of those trees. The fact that it happened reinforces Peter's words that "We must obey God rather than men!" (v. 29). Even actions in our secular occupations can have eternal consequences. God desires us to look to him as we choose what to do and say.

 Jesus, I know you died on that tree for me. Help my activities today to point to your resurrection victory.

Take a survey in your home to see what types of woods have been put to use there.

■ TRAITS OF EVIL

Jude 3-14: "These men are blemishes at your love feasts" (v. 12).

In his urgent call "to contend for the faith," Jude draws illustrations from history, literature and the natural world. A study of biblical and extrabiblical materials may be required for a clearer understanding of many of Jude's examples. His comparisons with natural phenomena still speak clearly to us today.

Clouds without rain and harvesttime trees with no fruit remain apt descriptions of those who never follow through with their commitment to Jesus. Those who attract undue attention to themselves still are likely to be waves that go to foam when they hit the shore. Others who impress us with programs and techniques for making life worthwhile may still parallel those in Jude's day who acted as wandering stars not linked with any bona fide constellation of faith.

Jude's warning concerned those who took advantage of the Christian life without making genuine commitments themselves. In our own time it may actually be more difficult than in early church times to distinguish those who hold a true faith from those who do not. Mass media, sales pitch techniques and bulk mail give us contact with an enormous number of persons who want the Christian community's blessing and support. By using Jude's description of the unfaithful men, we may have a good reference for revealing the internal motivations of some of those who ask for our support.

 Lord, make me faithful to your cause.

Look for additional examples in nature of godly and ungodly living.

■ SUSTAINING ALL THINGS

Heb. 1:1-12:   "The Son is the radiance of God's glory" (v. 3).

Faith makes the invisible visible to us. With it we have a window on history as the consistent report on the natures of both God and humankind. With it we have a door by which to meet the radiant Son of God face to face. Our faith also gives us the opportunity to believe that the visible world is sustained by the invisible God, and that adjacent to the visible realm is a spiritual realm of angels and beings that we have never seen.

Even so, sometimes it is difficult for us to accept the natural and the supernatural as equally real. Hebrews gives a mighty and magnificent description of Jesus' place in both worlds. Such a Scripture can lift us to a more perfect understanding of Christ's preeminence in both the earthly and the heavenly places. Our faith will be healthier, more dynamic and closer to the place that God holds open for us if we learn to take him at his word concerning things we cannot see.

 Lord, you laid the foundations of the earth, and the heavens are your handiwork. Create in me an awesome awareness of your omnipresence.

Take a quiet walk and consider that there is an unseen realm as well as an earthly one.

■ FRUIT OF EVERY KIND

Matt. 7:15-20:   "A good tree cannot bear bad fruit" (v. 18).

All flowering plants in a botanical sense produce "fruit." Depending on the plant, however, we are likely to call the end result a vegetable, a seed or a nut. Fruit is the ripened ovary of any flower. Again, we limit the botanical terminology in our daily usage. For us, "flowering trees" often are those landscape ornamentals such as cherry and crabapple. But, with few exceptions, all deciduous (or leaf-losing) trees are flowering, and thus fruit-bearing, plants.

Spring's the time to make a study of tree flowers. Some like the large flowers of the tulip tree will impress you with their beauty. Others that rely on wind pollination may be less conspicuous. Getting to know the trees' flowers and their fruits will give you a clearer understanding of the plants around you. And why not, for it is a principle that holds true in both a natural and a spiritual sense.

 Lord, help me to be more attentive to the fruit being produced around me, and let me choose to partake only of the good.

Learn the flower and the fruit of every tree on your block. Library books may be useful in learning more about both the native and the ornamental trees in your neighborhood.

■ REPRODUCTION POTENTIAL

Matt. 28:16-20: ". . . make disciples of all nations" (v. 19).

Eleven disciples heard the "Great Commission" directly from Jesus' lips, and over the centuries hundreds of thousands have come to believe in Christ.

In his booklet *Born to Reproduce* (Navpress, 1983), Dawson Trotman wrote that if each person who came to know Christ was faithful in bringing another to belief every half year, a church could grow from one person to 1,024 persons in just five years. At the end of 15½ years with such a rate of growth, 2,147,500,000 would populate that church. These figures, however, represent only potential and not actual happenings. Reproduction potential is amazingly high in most plants and animals as well.

Because of many factors such as disease and accidental deaths, populations do not skyrocket as the potentials might indicate they would. In the church, growth is slowed by the many believers who remain "babes in Christ." Most of these believers cannot lead others to Christ. Others are so unhealthy from the effects of sin that they are ineffective witnesses. Only persons who keep their faith strong are continuously able to bring others into the body of believers. Discipleship and evangelism both are important in the growth of the church. Each day we should be asking for the opportunity to "make disciples."

 Lord, I pray that *(a name of an unsaved friend)* will come to know you.

Figure out the reproductive potential of one tree by estimating the number of seeds it bears.

■ NIPPING THE BUD

James 1:13-18: "After desire has conceived, it gives birth to sin" (v. 15).

If you are surprised or discouraged by how quickly certain sins pull you down, take a critical look at the nature of your heart. It is likely that you will find the start of your problem there where desires are conceived and quietly expressed.

It is our responsibility to "nip sin in the bud" by repenting of wrong desires before they grow into sin. A better understanding of the growth of plants can encourage us to give our wrong thoughts over to God before they pervade our lives with damaging influences.

When you remove the tip of a growing stem, you actually remove the chemical control center that has been suppressing other stem growth. That is why geraniums, marigolds and many other flowers grow fuller and stronger when you trim them back. The removal of the natural leading bud gives small side stems the opportunity to grow.

When God speaks to you about removing a certain desire or entertained thought before it grows into sin, take God at his immediate word. By doing so, you will be removing the spiritual control center that has been suppressing your growing into a fuller and more hardy believer.

 Lord, make me sensitive and submissive to your pruning shears.

Cut back a spindly flower. Watch how quickly new and vigorous growth occurs.

■ WAITING

Rom. 8:18-23: "The creation waits in eager expectation" (v. 19).

Humankind at times has foolishly put its trust in the wholesomeness of the natural. Some have gone so far as to worship the life forms of earth. They have seen the sun, moon and other parts of creation as prototypes of perfect beauty, peace and harmony.

For all the loveliness and tranquility that nature shows, Christians must remember that the world has been utterly flawed by sin. Because of our own choices, every part of creation is living under the frustration of being less than God intended. Death and decay have the victory, and we have very little understanding as to what Christ really created the natural world to be.

But, we do have hope that in God's time he will show us the fullness of the redemptive work of Christ. Until then, in some mysterious way, we and creation both are waiting for Christ and his followers to take their rightful and victorious place. What a day that will be when Christ returns. Then we will experience the full revelation of God's glory and God's plan for creation and humankind.

 God, give me a greater sense of wonder that even creation is eagerly waiting for your return.

On a walk, look for ways that death and decay seem to claim the victory in life. Reflect on what the Garden of Eden must have been.

■ IMITATIONS OF CHRIST

Eph. 5:1-2: "Be imitators of God" (v. 1).

Many an insect's life is preserved by its ability to imitate. There are leafhoppers that look like thorns, walking sticks that look like twigs, moths that look like bark and butterflies that look like leaves. Despite such fascinating encounters with imitation in the natural world, nothing surpasses the possibility laid out by Paul's challenge in Ephesians.

His is an extraordinary exhortation. Humans should act like God. A partial understanding of this challenge may cause one to hope that Christianity will justify such natural inclinations as feeling and acting superior to others. But, Paul's challenge actually takes us to the opposite pole. Christ is our example of God on earth. The true mark of our imitation of the Holy One is "a life of love." This requires a complete emptying of our self and obedience to the Almighty One. The one who marks the way is Jesus Christ himself who became submissive even to death. Imitators in the natural world and in the human arena are everywhere. Unfortunately for humankind, there are too few who really accept the challenge to be "imitators of God."

 Lord, what a marvel it is that you should give us the opportunity to be like you. Help me to desire a "life of love" above all other ways.

Make a study of the camouflage and the warning coloration used by local animals.

■ DWELLING PLACES

Ps. 91:1-2: "He is my refuge" (v. 2).

In North America alone, there are 1500 different kinds of *galls*, those irregular growths in plants that protect and feed developing insects. Galls are interesting to look for because they come in so many shapes. In deciduous (or leaf-losing) forests, you may find the brown ping-pong-ball-size oak apple gall or the small hard oak bullet galls. In evergreen forests you might see spruce pineapple galls at the tips of branches. In fields you should be able to find one or more types of goldenrod galls. Leaf galls often appear on witchhazel, cherry and maple trees.

Galls form when an aphid, wasp or other flying insect lays its egg inside the plant tissue. This process irritates the plant and causes a deformation. Probably the most fantastic thing is that each gall maker confines its activities to only one plant species. It is uncertain how the insect makes the "right choice" in finding its plant. But, when it does, the gall that forms does much to provide for and protect the otherwise defenseless insect young.

God promises to be our defense. More often than not, we cannot give a detailed explanation of how God will accomplish this in our lives. Our need for protection from both spiritual and physical attacks is great. Yet, like a gall-maker, his presence can actually produce a refuge where none existed. "Never will I leave you; never will I forsake you" (Heb. 13:5).

 Lord, I take refuge in your promises and your constant presence.

Look for different galls and learn about the gall makers responsible for them.

■ AT THE RIGHT PLACE

Mal. 4:1-3: ". . . that day that is coming will set them on fire" (v. 1).

Our earth maintains a life-sustaining track around one particular star, our sun, with its surface temperature of 9,900 degrees Fahrenheit. It is not difficult to imagine what a fiery furnace we would face if our tiny blue-and-green planet moved closer to its immense source of heat. On the other hand, the earth would become a frozen wasteland if our track moved farther out. The miracle of being at just the right distance from the sun is something that we take for granted every day.

As believers, we have been placed by God in life-giving orientation with his very being. "Because of the Lord's great love, we are not consumed," says Lam. 3:22. It is only because of his mercy that we can bask in his presence instead of living in the dark void of our own sinfulness. This blessing of being in just the right place comes because of Christ's completed work. The same God who brought light into the universe became man and lived out his perfection in an earthly form, so that we actually could see his face. Yet, someday (as the Malachi passage warns) every human will experience the full unleashing of God's power.

 You, Lord, are all-powerful, all-knowing, all-righteous. Yet, today, I rejoice because you allow me to seek your face. Humbly, I give you thanks and praise.

Read an article or a book that gives facts about our solar system.

■ HANGING ON

Heb. 12:11: "No discipline seems pleasant at the time. . . ."

The beautiful colors of autumn are a sign of death. Brilliant yellows and golds, which have been in some leaves all summer, can be seen only when the leaves stop producing life-sustaining chlorophyll. Autumn reds and purples often form only when the leaves are no longer productive parts of the plants. For a little while the forest can sustain this gaudy show. But soon stiff breezes and chilly rains cause the leaves to drop. The leaves' downfall comes easily, in part because of the thin abscission layers that have been forming between leaf stems and twigs. Separated from the tree, the leaves cannot survive for long.

Life's temporal pleasures are much like autumn leaves. They appear so attractive that we hardly can resist them. Yet, the Bible warns that we must not replace our discipline in Christ with what seems to be a more glamorous style of living. No matter how comfortable and right they seem, life-styles that are not anchored in Christ already carry the mark of death. Like dying leaves, the signs of doom may be attractive instead of dull. Yet, we must remember that just as the leaf cannot survive apart from the tree that formed it, we cannot find life apart from the God who made us.

 Lord, help me to live the kind of disciplined life that produces a "harvest of righteousness."

Each tree in the autumn forest contributes certain colors. Learn to know what colors are displayed by common tree species.

■ LOWLY THINGS

1 Cor. 1:27-31: "God chose the weak things of the world to shame the strong" (v. 27).

Mosses occupy unique places. Often they grow where other plants cannot. Sometimes their presence starts the soil-making process that eventually invites other plants. Though they can produce their own food, they lack a true vascular system. Still, the simple mosses have complex life-styles.

The green moss plants we normally see are gametophytes. Sperm and egg are united during the gametophyte stage. A second stage, the sporophyte, then is formed. Inside the tip of the sporophyte, spores ripen. When they are released, they grow into threadlike protonema which eventually produce new leafy gametophytes. Such is the life cycle of a "low form" of plant life!

We ignore the complexities represented by other things, too. What workings allow the ant to crawl, the bumblebee to fly, the bird to develop within its egg? Such mysteries have baffled observers for years. When the simple things of nature confound the intellect, nature designates no spokesperson to explain them. When the happenings of Christianity stir questions from observers, however, God desires that we give them answers. Each of us has a responsibility in this, for as 1 Peter 3:15 aptly puts it: "Always be prepared to give an answer to everyone who asks you to give reason for the hope that you have. But do this with gentleness and respect. . . ."

Lord, help me to prepare a reason for my hope.

Look for moss gametophytes and sporophytes.

■ EVERY ANIMAL

Ps. 50:1-11: "I know every bird in the
mountains. . ." (v. 11).

This psalm gives a glimpse of God's omniscience.
Imagine having the ability to see all the mountain
peaks of the world at once. Then recognize that God's
ability far exceeds even this. God knows the location
and the movement of every bird on those peaks. And
if every bird, then every insect, too. And if every
insect, then also every virus.

In this manner of thinking, are we exaggerating the
interest that God has in his creatures? Probably not,
for Christ himself said "even the very hairs of your
head are all numbered" (Matt. 10:30). Our
understanding of God's intimacy with creation should
help us to rest in him. If we are ill, God knows the
causes. If we are exposed to disease, God knows the
location of each bacterium. If we struggle with a
handicap, God knows the functioning of each abnormal
cell. This leaves us with no option but to express our
inner needs to God and trust that he can accomplish
his perfect will in us. Let us continue to strive to
know our heavenly Father as Asaph did: "He is the
Mighty One, God, the Lord" (v. 1).

 Mighty One, you know all about me. God, you
hear the inner longings of my heart. Lord, you
are the only one in whom I can trust. From
morning to morning I will seek your face.

**Participate in an annual bird count with a local
Audubon Society chapter or start a life list that
records the birds you have seen.**

■ ANT LESSON

Prov. 6:6-8: "Go to the ant . . . consider its ways and be wise" (v. 6).

The harvester ants, to which Solomon referred, actually work all summer long to harvest grain kernels which they then hull and store in underground chambers. As many as 90,000 individuals may live in one colony, and their food caches are significant enough that the *Talmud* specified that ant grain chambers belonged to the gleaners and not to the field owners.

More than 12,000 species of ants populate the world. Almost every ant you see is an infertile female. These "workers" really earn their name by constantly collecting food, caring for the queen, running the nursery and building living quarters.

It seems impossible that such a small creature could venture forth to work and then find its way back home. It seems equally amazing that harmony and coordination would be present among such a vast number of tiny organisms. Studies show that ants seem to have well developed senses of smell, taste and feel. These give them a greater ability to work together. They may even use light polarization to determine direction from the rays of the sun.

From our point of view, it seems that ants would not be able to maintain the life-style that they do. In truth, the ant is perfectly suited to its position. If we let him, God can make us perfectly suited to our calling, too.

 Lord, just as you have perfectly suited the ant for its duties, assure me that, with your help, I can live each day for you.

Spend some time this week observing ants.

■ CAUGHT IN COBWEBS

Job 8:13-15: ". . . what he relies on is a spider's web. . ." (v. 14).

Though most of us want to keep our distance from them, spiders have a beneficial role in insect pest control. Overcoming our aversion to these eight-legged creatures can open a new area of interesting observations. Spiders can be divided into two major groups—those that hunt and those that build webs.

Spiderweb study can almost be considered a form of art appreciation. If you look around your neighborhood, you'll probably find the spiral webs of the *Epeira* spiders, the dustcatching webs of the *Dictynas*, and the trampolines of the *Agalenas*. Each of these has a special lesson to teach in keeping us free from the cobwebs of sin.

In the morning sun, the *Epeira's* round web can string dew drops like expensive jewels. One touch to the supporting threads, however, shows the bright choker to be a deadly snare across a wide path. It should remind us to stay away from things that glimmer without any spiritual "gold." The *Dictyna's* sticky web should make us leery of collecting possessions that gather only dust and not eternal rewards. Finally, the *Agalena's* lacy trap can reflect earth-bound priorities and greed. At first such a web appears to be a smooth, firm foundation. Suddenly, we find ourselves within reach of the deadly cobweb-maker, Satan, and unable to come loose from the web.

 Loving God, help me to see spiritual snares for what they really are, and to focus on things that have eternal value.

See how many spiders you can find outside in 10 minutes.

■ OUT OF THE CLOSET

Ps. 39:6-11: ". . . you consume their wealth like a moth. . ." (v. 11).

Cloth moths can be found anywhere in the world where woolen fabrics are stored. The larvae that do the actual damage are small enough to live inconspicuously between the threads, but the holes they make are certainly conspicuous. The adult moths that emerge from the pupae of these larvae are small, thin-winged varieties. Unlike many other moths, cloth moths are attracted to darkness instead of to light. For this reason, prolonged exposure to sunlight can prevent moth damage in fabrics.

Jesus warns us not to store up riches that can be destroyed by moths (Matt. 6:19-21). Because of the nature of the cloth moth, we might be able to guess that Christ was referring to the access possessions that we so often horde or covet. As a method of obeying Jesus' command, we might find it helpful to expose all of our possessions to his light. By bringing them "out of the closet" of our selfishness, we can rely on his help to discern our real needs. Whatever nonessentials we find in our search can be put to better use by relying on his leadings. When our housecleaning is done, we'll have assurance that our heart is more in heaven and that our possessions are in their right places on earth.

 Lord, give me a maturity that puts you above every earthly possession.

Check your closets for the presence of cloth moths—as well as for items that could be put to better use elsewhere.

FINDING THE WAY

Isa. 30:19-21: "This is the way; walk in it" (v. 21).

Bird migration has fascinated nature observers for centuries. Migratory birds have an inborn sense of direction. This ability to "find the way" cannot be attributed to learned behavior since birds that never have migrated previously still fly along traditional flyways.

Observations of many types of migratory species show that certain birds orient themselves by stars, by landmarks and/or by gravitational pull. The fact that one small blue patch of sky is enough to give direction may indicate that some birds respond to the polarization of light. For all that has been learned, however, no one can clearly say exactly how birds find their way despite all types of environmental conditions and obstacles.

No one, perhaps, could summarize the spiritual lesson taught by bird migration better than William Cullen Bryant did in his famous poem "To a Waterfowl":

> He, who, from zone to zone,
> Guides through the boundless sky thy certain flight,
> In the long way that I must trace alone,
> Will lead my steps aright.

Expect guidance from the Lord as you travel with him today.

 Thank you, God, that though you are unseen you are always there.

Learn the migratory habits of the birds that live in your area.

■ A THIRD WAY

Prov. 3:5-12: "This will bring health . . ." (v. 8).

Pain, fear or stress in mammals can cause a release of adrenalin. The presence of this hormone brings about many bodily changes such as a rise in the blood pressure, an acceleration of the heartbeat, an increase in oxygen consumption and a resistance to fatigue. Biology books sometimes call such responses fight-or-flight reactions because of the possibility that adrenalin helps animals to either strengthen their fight or to hasten their flight. In nature, there are only two normal reactions to stress. The hunted rabbit runs. The cornered tiger fights. Whether the response is to "fight" or to take "flight" is part of the innate behavior of each species.

Pain, fear and emotional stress in humans can cause the same biological reactions of "fight or flight." Our heart races. Our pupils dilate. Goosebumps come out on our flesh. We feel tense in our stomachs. As with animals, our immediate, ingrained response may be either to lash out at the cause of our distress or to flee from it in fear. As Christians, however, we have a third and infinitely better way of coping with adrenalin-releasing situations. That way is trust. Putting our full trust in God can protect our bodies from the documented wearing effects of worry and stress. In a real sense, trusting in God can bring "health" to our bodies and "nourishment" to our bones.

 Lord, I trust in you.

Watch for the "flight" and "fight" responses in nature.

■ A FELLOWSHIP OF BELIEVERS

1 Thess. 5:10-18: "Live in peace with each other" (v. 13).

Many types of animals travel in groups. In the bird world alone, you can find "charms" of goldfinches, "exhaltations" of larks, "rafts" of ducks, "wings" of plovers and "whitenesses" of swans. While methods of synchronizing activity and of communicating within flocks remain largely unknown to human observers, the benefits of such groups seem apparent. Group living offers protection for the individual. The young, in many cases, are raised within the safety of large numbers of adults. Energy is conserved and feeding time is maximized when the work of individual birds directly benefits the entire flock. The lead goose, for example, sets up a wake that makes flight easier for those following in the V-formation. Alert sentinels in groups such as gulls provide protection for others who are resting or eating.

Group life for the Christian is essential, too. We refer to our corporateness as our "church" or our "fellowship." Unlike the obscure group dynamics in nature, the workings within Christian gatherings are stated clearly in the Scriptures. The passages in 1 Thessalonians, for example, highlight many of the elements of healthy fellowship groups. Prayerfully consider Paul's instructions here. Are you doing your full share to make your fellowship sound and productive?

 God, you have made me a part of (*name your fellowship*). Thank you for this group.

Watch the marvelous ways in which flocks of birds move and travel together.

■ PERSEVERE!

1 Peter 1:13-16: ". . . prepare your minds for action; be self-controlled . . ." (v. 13).

How much we accomplish in our walk of faith largely depends on how willing we are to persevere. The scriptures are well seasoned with admonitions to hold fast to the good and shun what is evil. These instructions only put into words what we already know from experience: the Christian life is not an easy one.

Nature provides some interesting examples of perseverence. Though a hummingbird weighs only one-eighth of an ounce, it makes a 500-mile migration flight in just 10 hours. Though the monarch butterfly has a mere four-inch wingspan, it might flutter more than 2000 miles to its wintering grounds.

To our way of thinking, such creatures would be better off if their physical makeups were different or if their tasks were smaller. We have a tendency to wish things were different in our own realm of experiences, too. The consistency with which the hummingbird, the monarch, and many of nature's other creatures carry through despite enormous odds, however, reminds us that we are strengthened to go the whole way through life with God. Animals succeed, though their only motivation is instinct and their only reward is the survival of their kind. How much more we should be willing to persevere, for our motivation is Christ himself and our reward is an eternal crown.

 Lord, I have decided to follow Jesus, and I will not turn back.

Learn the migration patterns of the monarch butterfly or of a common migratory animal in your area.

■ TRANSFORMATION

2 Cor. 5:11-21: ". . . the old has gone, the new has come!" (v. 17).

All summer long gossamer-winged insects grace the lakeshore. Starting in May, troupes of mayflies perform whirling mating flights. Later, the scene gives way to caddisflies and stoneflies swarming around lakeshore lights.

Go to the lake in winter, however, and you will find no insect activities—unless you dip down to explore the lake bottom. With a cup, a sieve and much patience, you may be able to retrieve live specimens of every pretty summer insect that flitted about the lake. But, without a guidebook, it will be difficult to know what you have caught, for the winter side of each of these insects is dull and drab. If you didn't know that metamorphosis would soon transform them into airborne adults, you'd have reason to believe that such creatures were permanently bound to a dim existence on the murky bottom.

Because of sin, each of us starts out being "bogged down" by life, too. Perhaps someone you know who has not accepted the saving work of Jesus Christ may say to you that unfairness, selfish ambition or mortality are the intrinsic trademarks of human existence. At such a moment, ask God to help you share the transformation that has taken place in your own life. Perhaps your testimony will help this person to find a new heaven-bound life in Christ.

 Lord, help me to share my transformation experience with others.

Try collecting and identifying immature aquatic insects.

■ A CLEAR PATHWAY

1 Peter 4:1-7: "Therefore be clear minded and self-controlled so that you can pray" (v. 7).

Meadow voles (sometimes called meadow mice) are so common that 10,000 of them might live in one acre of field. Because of their abundance, they are a favorite food of many birds of prey and meat-eating mammals. The voles' best means of defense is the neat system of pathways that they maintain through the grass. Continually, these runways are cleaned and trimmed. No obstructions are allowed to form. Then, when an attack comes, the little creatures can be sure of a clear escape route.

We should tend our prayer and devotional life as closely as the meadow vole tends its paths. Our natural inclination may be to pray and study only when we're in a pinch and know we can't handle things without God's help. The truth of the matter is that prayer and Bible study should be top priorities every day, even when things are going well. By carrying through on these responsibilities, we will gain the blessing of having an open communications channel with God. Then, when trials descend like a hawk upon us, we will be confident of the pathway that takes us to our hiding place in Christ.

 Lord, I know that undisciplined and slothful living are less than your best for me. Guide me in the use of every day.

Look for meadow voles and their pathways in fields and vacant lots.

■ NO LOOSE ENDS

1 Cor. 3:10-15: ". . . fire will test the quality of each man's work" (v. 13).

Each bird species has a unique style of nest. Each species uses different materials, seeks out a specific habitat and prefers a certain nesting height. Song sparrows and orioles, for example, both build with hair. Yet, the former tucks its tightly lined cup in some low bush, while the latter hangs its silvery purselike structure out on a high branch. Some birds even have trademarks for their housing projects. For the great-crested flycatcher, the *piece de resistance* is a bit of snake skin; for the catbird, it's a decoration of grapevine.

Regardless of the style, the function of the nest remains the same. It provides a safe environment for eggs and the young.

Life offers different materials, living situations and events to each of us. God does not expect our accomplishments and tasks to match those of any others. Often we make a mess of things by trying to live out another person's strong points and spiritual gifts. We can find personal contentment and harmony by turning our daily activities over to God. God can weave the circumstances of our life into a beautiful masterpiece if we give him the freedom to pattern things after his own design.

 God, sometimes my life seems to be all knots and loose ends. Take over, Lord, and make me after your own design.

Look for (but don't remove) different types of bird nests.

■ OUT OF SIGHT

Ps. 32:1-7: "You are my hiding place" (v. 7).

Those who frequent the field and forest soon learn that animals aren't easily seen. Yet, there are hiding places everywhere. As a hiker, you may be surrounded by many creatures—all at arm's length and completely out of sight. Looking for a creature's ingenious technique of concealment can be as fascinating as finding the animal itself. Such a search may draw you down to the ground to see how the trapdoor spider closes its funnel with a camouflaged lid. Or, you may find the sandy funnel of an immature antlion who is buried at the bottom ready to devour unwary ants that fall into its hole. A fawn might lie motionless in the patchy woodlot sunlight right in front of you while above your head a sleepy owl blends in with the gnarled limb on which it rests.

It is comforting to know that God welcomes us when we need a refuge. We can draw near to God when we feel like hiding our face from others because of hurt, disappointment, embarrassment or shame. God knows every aspect of our painful encounter so we can find hope in the fact that God accepts us, forgives us and protects us within the confines of his perfect will. Nothing can separate God and those who have been redeemed by the death of his Son on the cross. Even when the world comes to an end, we will have our hiding place in God.

 Draw your arms around me, loving God, so that I can rest in you.

Spend a half-hour in an outdoor setting looking for animals that are in hiding places.

■ EARTHLY MELODIES

Ps. 98:4-9: ". . . make music to the Lord" (v. 5).

Over the centuries, humans have worshiped God with a variety of melodies and musical instruments. In addition to these manmade offerings of praise, the Scriptures lead us to believe that nature presents its own forms of music before the Creator-God. Seas clap against the shore. Leaves rustle in the wind. Bees hum busily all day long. Thunder rumbles between the mountain peaks. Listen for one of nature's many symphonies, and thank God that you can enjoy its loveliness with him.

> All thy works with joy surround thee,
> Earth and Heaven reflect thy rays,
> Stars and angels sing around thee,
> Center of unbroken praise.
> Field and forest, vale and mountain,
> Flow'ry meadow, flashing sea,
> Chanting bird, and flowing fountain
> Call us to rejoice in thee.
> —"Joyful, Joyful We Adore Thee," by Henry Van Dyke with courtesy of Charles Scribner's Sons

 Almighty One, with the chorus of earth and heaven, I bring praises to you.

Tonight seek out a symphony of frogs beside a pond or the song of winds through the trees.

■ FLAMING TONGUES

James 3:5-6:   "Consider what a great forest is set on fire by a small spark" (v. 5).

Sometimes when a tree is felled, the scars of a long-ago forest fire are exposed. A tree's life is in jeopardy each time a fire ravages its home. Trees that survive having portions of their bark burned soon develop scar tissue along the edges of the wound. Year after year, bark continues to enclose the opening. If enough years pass, normal growth rings may start to form again around the entire tree. This resumed normal growth completely envelops the former scar. It remains a tight secret that can be exposed only by delving deeply into the wood.

James says that the tongue is like an evil fire, taking licks at others and bringing destruction to itself. Counselors often trace the maladjustments in adulthood back to hurts that were received when the person was a child. Over the years, the scar caused by verbal singeing may appear as normal growth. Its weakness and inferiorities are likely to surface, however, when relationships start going deep.

Within the church we should find a ministry of healing for such wounds. Unlike the trees, we need not bear scars from flaming tongues forever. Let us be cautious about words and conciliatory in our deeds.

 Lord, help me not to fear the exposure of my hurt. I know there is forgiveness and healing in your presence.

When sorting firewood, keep an eye open for signs of forest fire scars in the logs.

◼ ROOTED IN LOVE

Eph. 3:14-21: ". . . being rooted and established in love. . ." (v. 17).

The mature tree is a fantastic organism. An old oak, for example, is likely to bear a magnificent crown composed of far-reaching branches, thousands of food-producing leaves and hundreds of acorns. All this is supported by a thick trunk made up of living transportation tissue and dead supportive wood. Everything above ground is supported by perhaps several hundred miles of convoluted roots.

As the tree ages, the essential life processes of such a venerable landmark continue in the same manner as in its tender youth. Water is absorbed molecule by molecule through the root hairs. Minerals and sugar move up and down the trunk, cell by cell. Thousands of gallons of water are transpired annually by the leaves, leaving molecule by molecule through stomata (the guarded leaf openings).

Paul seemed to have a vision of the church as a "family tree" when he prayed his glorious prayer for the believers at Ephesus. He saw each Christian there as part of the total outgrowth of God's will. He prayed with the knowledge that they had to be rooted in Christ, for through Jesus alone can come the spiritual nourishment needed to produce a healthy and far-reaching crown. Even greater than this Ephesus "tree" is the one that includes the church of all believers.

 Lord, I thank you for my place on your "family tree."

Have a quiet time this week under a large old tree.

■ CURSED BEINGS

Gal. 3:10-14:   "Christ redeemed us from the curse. . ." (v. 13).

Poison ivy seems to incur everyone's wrath. Yet, like so many other irritating natural organisms, the plant does have redeeming qualities. The waxy white berries provide food for many songbirds during the long harsh winters. The three-parted leaves add excellent colors to the fall foliage display. Still, most of us would think that these are not enough to bring esteem to the poison ivy plant.

Worse than any troublesome natural organism is the heart of man. Jeremiah 17:9 states that "The heart is deceitful above all things and beyond cure." Even the Almighty God could find no way to remove the rightful curse that we were to receive for our evil nature. Yet, God still was willing to reconcile us to himself by letting Christ take on the irremovable punishment for our sin.

Let the so-often-cursed poison ivy vines that cover so many trees be reminders to us that the Holy Son of God hung on a tree to take away our punishment for sin. We have no redeeming qualities apart from those that are hidden in the new life he gives us when we believe.

 God, forgive me when I think I have redeeming qualities that make me righteous apart from Christ's redemptive work in me.

Learn to recognize poison ivy and its hairy climbing vines. From a safe distance, look for its fruits and watch which animals use them as food.

■ ALIENS IN THE LAND

Ex. 23:9:   "Do not oppress an alien."

God's chosen people spent much of their time living as aliens among foreign tribes and in strange lands. At times, God used other cultures to humble and bring judgment to the people of God. Often, however, God allowed the chosen ones to prosper and thrive even when they were aliens in the land. Their good fortune and strength often provided evidence that God truly was with Israel.

Wildflower field guides sometimes use the word "alien" to designate plants that are not native. Many alien plants in this country are thriving weeds. For various reasons, these plants have been able to out-compete native species under certain conditions. It is interesting to learn the names of alien plants and to study the characteristics that make them so hardy. Even though we do not appreciate most of them, they can help us to remember that God can sustain and bless us even in foreign settings.

As Christians we are to be sojourners on the earth. We are citizens of the kingdom of God who continue to dwell on earth for a little while. Let us ask God's blessing on our living here so that we may be witnesses for that eternal kingdom that is to come.

 Lord, remind me that my citizenship is in heaven.

Find out which of the plants in your neighborhood are "alien" ones.

■ DEVOTED PARTNERS

Rom. 12:9-13: "Share with God's people who are in need" (v. 13).

Lichens are fine examples in nature of two organisms working together. Any lichens you find on rocks and trees are a combination of two plants—a fungus and an alga. Because the fungus cannot make food for itself, it depends on the photosynthesis of the alga. On the other hand, the alga cannot live alone in a dry environment apart from the protection that the fungus gives. Some scientists point out that lichens may not truly exemplify *mutualism* (a relationship in which both partners benefit) because algae can live on their own under certain conditions. Perhaps, then, they say, the fungi actually confine algae only to meet their own nutritional needs.

Regardless of the type of relationship lichens display in a scientific sense, their relationship teaches a fine lesson. Because of their unique life-style, they are capable of growing on barren rock. Their activity there erodes the rock and paves the way for mosses and rooted plants.

As partners in the church, we will not always personally benefit from the sharing we are called to do. Sometimes we must actually confine our own interests in the interest of serving others. The practice of putting others first, however, always benefits the total church organism. Acts in a spirit of servitude make the church strong, harmonious and able to thrive in conditions where no secular partnerships can.

 Lord, whom do you want me to serve today?

Look for lichens on your next outdoor excursion.

■ ON YOUR TOES

Hab. 3:16-19: ". . . he makes my feet like the feet of a deer" (v. 19).

Habakkuk's trust was tested to the limit. Prophecy told him that destruction was coming to his people. In the long run, he knew, good would be the result of God's execution of justice. The immediate effects, however, would be tragedy, suffering and death. Only God could give him the confidence needed to endure, and not only to endure but also to have victory. Because he knew his God as well as the future, Habakkuk found himself "on his toes" with anticipation of the glory soon to come. He saw himself as a deer, swift and strong enough to reach high ground.

Deer are fast and graceful largely because they walk on their toes. Some types of North American deer can maintain speeds of 25 miles per hour for several miles. They can leap 20 feet without apparent effort. Being "on their toes" is their assurance of attaining safety from their enemies. In a spiritual sense, it can be our assurance, too. Each moment let us be ready to match our faith with our circumstances. By being alert and "on our toes," we can always make our way with God's help to the high point of praise.

 Almighty God, despite what this day holds, let me be swift to find refuge in you.

Learn to know the shape of deer footprints and try tracking a deer through moist soil or snow.

■ IN THE CLOUDS

Rev. 1:7-8: "Look, he is coming with the clouds" (v. 8).

In the Peanuts comic strip by Charles Shultz, Lucy asks her companions what they see in the clouds. Linus reports that, among other things, he has seen a representation of the stoning of Stephen. Charlie Brown, in turn, reluctantly confesses that all he has been looking at up above are a "duckie and a horsie."

There may be truth in the idea that our life focus is revealed, to some extent, by what we see in the clouds. In 1803 a London pharmacist devised the terminology for the three major types of clouds: cirrus, cumulus and stratus. Later in the nineteenth century, almanacs started to carry lists of reliable weather indicators that included the "course and color of clouds" as worthy characteristics.

Current books on cloud formations can help you to guess at the weather changes. These resources teach you to recognize common cloud types and atmospheric conditions. Studying the clouds can make you more than an amateur weather prognosticator. The activity can serve to remind you that someday you will witness a life-changing event taking place in the sky. As the Bible promises, one day we will see Christ himself returning in the clouds.

 Jesus, let the beauty of the sky today remind me that you are coming again.

Make it a practice to look up at the clouds at least once each day. Learn to recognize the common cloud formations in your area.

■ A LAYER OF CONFIDENCE

Isa. 50:4-8: ". . . I set my face like flint" (v. 7).

Mountain peaks and ridges often are formed when rocks of different hardnesses are exposed to the same external forces. In the hills of Judea and in much of the Sinai, flint is the material of the high places. Flint gains this prominence because it is withstanding the erosional forces that are wearing away the softer limestones and chalks.

Isaiah could not have given us a clearer word-picture of determination than that of setting our face "like flint" against whatever eroding forces come our way. Such a determination to be righteous is especially important in our day, when ungodliness is rapidly encroaching even upon such worthy endeavors as literature and art.

Any stand you take for a righteous cause may make you uncomfortably conspicuous. In such a circumstance it is good to know that the Holy Spirit will undergird you as you hold fast to the word of God. Watch out for a "holier than thou" attitude that can develop as you interact with those who oppose you. But, don't be afraid to be set apart by others because of your peculiar acts of love and kindness during harsh confrontation. Your tranquility will point to the source of your inner strength. Because of your actions, others, who are watching you from a distance, may actually be won to Christ.

 Christ, when times are rough remind me of your strength and peace.

Take a field trip to a place that has been patterned by erosion.

■ GOD IS MY ROCK

Psalm 62: "(God) alone is my rock and my salvation" (v. 2).

By turning over a rock in the woodlands you might uncover a salamander, the nursery chamber of an ant hill or the unseen entrance to a chipmunk home. In the nation's dry Southwest, a rock cluster might protect the chuckwalla, a lizard that actually puffs out its body to fit tightly in its rocky hiding place. On the other hand, your search might scare up a snake or yellow jackets from their underground homes.

Being careful with the use of your hands is the first rule in conducting a search for the many interesting creatures that rely on rocky homes. The second rule of such a search is to replace the rocks once you have looked under them. This practice ensures that the ground squirrel will have a possible refuge from the swooping hawk and that the centipede will find a place to rest. If we are not considerate of the animals that use rocky refuges, we can thoughtlessly tear apart their homes during our casual search for wildlife.

As you train yourself to find the animals that dwell among rocks, consider your own need for security. By choosing God as your spiritual fortress, you have come upon a secure "rock." Christ can never be overthrown by any philosophy or form of criticism, nor can any force take the companionship of Jesus from you.

 Jesus, you are my rock of confidence and my shelter in life's storms.

Enjoy a picnic supper on a rocky outcrop while you watch the activities of small animals living there.

■ WITHIN HEARING RANGE

Deut. 30:19-20: "This day I call heaven and earth as witnesses" (v. 19).

Noise is a part of our life. Car horns honk, radios blare, heavy equipment pounds away. From the moment our alarm clock goes off until we fall asleep in front of the late night TV news, our day is filled with sounds. Noise pollution is a real concern in our technological age.

Noise, however, is not an invention of the twentieth century. If you read your Bible with a keen sensitivity to the historical settings, you can almost hear the clatter of chariot wheels, the shouts of the crowds, the musical instruments of the priests. One of the most magnificent sounds in civilization must have come soon after the Israelites entered the promised land under Joshua's leadership. With half of the tribes on Mount Gerizim and half of the tribes on Mount Ebal, Joshua read God's covenant.

Imagine the Scriptures echoing back and forth across the open valley and over the sounds of crying babies, bleating livestock, and fidgety children. On that day, heaven and earth witnessed the fact that every Israelite had heard the word of the Lord. Now it became the responsibility of each individual to act on what had been said and heard.

 God, you formed the universe with your creative Word. You saved my life from destruction with your forgiving Word. Heaven and earth are your witnesses. Thank you, Lord.

Plan an outdoor church activity to dramatize the reading of the Law as it is recorded in Josh. 8:30-35.

■ WHO SEES THE WIND?

John 3:8-13: "The wind blows wherever it pleases" (v. 8).

W̲ho has seen the wind?
  Neither I nor you:
But when the leaves hang trembling
  The wind is passing through.

—Christina Rossetti

Perhaps bits of this childhood poem stir within you as you walk through fields or forests on a breezy day.

The air you are breathing this minute was over a different geographical location yesterday; by tomorrow it will be gone again. While it stays with you, it is likely to impart the temperature and the humidity that it derived from someplace else on the globe. When all is said and done, most of us are not so much concerned with the movement of the wind as we are with its effects on us in the form of weather.

God's spirit is, indeed, like the wind. It comes from God's habitation and brings with it the very nature of himself. Even as Christians, we may not be able to explain sufficiently this third person of the trinity theologically or explain his activities with words. But we sense God's presence, like the wind's, as God envelopes us.

 Come, Holy Spirit, blow through the windows of my heart.

Familiarize yourself with the Beaufort wind scale, an easy-to-use guide that allows you to approximate wind speed by observing the movement of everyday objects such as branches and smoke. This scale may be found in meteorological handbooks and encyclopedias.

■ AN OVERVIEW OF LIFE

Jer. 23:24: " 'Do not I fill heaven and earth?'
declares the Lord."

Vistas are a reward to those who hike mountain
trails. Well planned mountain pathways have clearcuts
maintained to give you views of the landscape
stretching out before you. Binoculars, compass and
topographic map can increase your enjoyment at an
overlook because, with them, you can actually locate
familiar features in the valley below. The appearance
of well-known landmarks and their relationship to one
another often is surprising when viewed from a
mountaintop.

God has a vista on the life of each of us. Because of
our human limitations, we can go through only one
valley of despair or up only one mountain of joy at a
time. But our omniscient God knows the entire
landscape of our lives. What's more, God does not
serve only as a passive observer who watches from a
distance. By the Spirit God draws close to us on each
leg of our journey. God's Spirit becomes our constant
companion and guide.

 Look up Psalm 139 and make it your own
personal prayer to God today.

A soil conservation officer, park staff person or forest
ranger can tell you how to obtain detailed
topographical maps of a given area. For practice in
compass reading and map work, get involved with an
orienteering group.

■ BEING LIFTED UP

James 4:10: "Humble yourselves before the Lord, and he will lift you up."

Hannah Hurnard, author of *Wayfarer in the Land* (Tyndale, 1976), was a missionary in the Holy Land. While there, she reflected on the contrast between the seemingly unchanging mountains near Jerusalem and the small, temporal communities built upon them. "The villages themselves were so small and comparatively frail," she wrote, "while the hills so immovably, so calmly and majestically, bore up without strain or weariness, everything built or growing or supported on them. Was not God's strength just like that?" (p. 134).

It is good to remember her words, for it is easy to let our church work become a mountainous burden on us. We surely are taking the wrong approach to things if temporal tasks—like planning a Christmas social or a wedding reception—pressure us to the point where we no longer find joy in our service to God.

When you feel the pressure coming, step back and let God lift you up for a look at events from his point of view.

 Faithful God, help me to sort out my commitments to the church and to others in the light of your love.

Explore a deserted mining camp or summer resort, and let the desolation of the once-active community remind you of the insignificance of even your "most important" projects.

■ MOUNTAINTOP EXPERIENCES

Psalm 121:   "I lift up my eyes to the hills. . ." (v. 1).

The Bible is full of "mountaintop experiences." On Mount Ararat, the ark with Noah's household and the animals came to rest. On Mount Moriah, the hill on which the temple of Jerusalem would be built, Abraham went to sacrifice his son Isaac. On Horeb, Moses saw the burning bush, and at this same place the Law was given. On verdant Mount Hermon, Christ was transfigured.

It is interesting that this last event occurred on Hermon, the most holy place of those who worshiped Baal. Each of the Bible's mountaintop events has at least one thing in common—the place became sacred *because* of the happenings that God orchestrated there. This is in sharp contrast to the neighboring Canaanites' human attempts to make high places holy by soliciting the response of Baal through the rites performed there.

The God of Abraham, Isaac and Jacob still comes to men and women, touching them with various supernatural encounters that momentarily transform ordinary portions of the earth into "holy ground." Be sensitive to the Lord's nearness to you, for the Lord desires to visit you again and again.

 Lord, I can make no place sacred on my own, but you, O Christ, can transform any place into a sanctuary worthy of an encounter with God.

Plan a retreat in a mountain setting. Spend several hours there alone with God.

■ HEWN FROM THE ROCK

Isa. 51:1-3: "Look to the rock from which you were cut" (v. 1).

When I was a teenager, I toured the huge quarry in Barre, Vermont, and to this day I see a little bit of beautiful New England in every granite cemetery marker that has been brought to my state. Even though the stones are polished now and far removed from the bedrock that formed them, they serve to remind me of the summers that I lived near their source.

Christians, too, should represent the bedrock of their faith. On the first day of a job, I once asked the secretary (in a private moment) if she was a Christian. Some peculiar type of kinship had developed immediately upon my being introduced to her. She smiled warmly and said, "Yes, and I had already guessed that you were a Christian, too."

What a blessed way to live! What a privilege to be placed like "living stones" in the way of life! When we sense our calling to build in others a foundation for faith, we can rejoice in the mission of being "bits" of heaven to the peoples of the earth. Regardless of the importance of your daily work as judged by secular standards, believe that you have significance because of the Rock from which you have been hewn.

 Thank you, God, for the possibility of displaying your characteristics in my life.

Visit a quarry to learn about the geology and removal of valuable types of stone.

■ NOT JUST KID STUFF

Gen. 9:8-17: "I have set my rainbow in the clouds" (v. 13).

Rainbows make great decorations for children's rooms, but we're missing the boat (literally) if we consider God's sign of the covenant only in its pleasant light. It should be remembered that, apart from the ark's passengers, no other creatures survived the devastation. Such events are not easily reconciled in our minds with a God who is presented as infinitely loving and tenderhearted. Our God is the same Sovereign One who stood by while thousands of Hebrew boys were killed at the time of Moses' birth and, later, after Jesus's birth. In light of such atrocities, can we still trust the God who put the rainbow in the sky?

The answer is an unequivocal *yes*. For God's faithfulness has been proved by God's making a way for righteousness even through earth's darkness hours. God brought about redemption for humankind even though wickedness threatened, at every turn, to defeat that plan.

Most physical science books will remind you that to see a rainbow you must stand with the storm in front of you and the sun at your back. Only the Bible, however, can assure us that we will live with Christ to see his final victory by facing the struggle before us with the Son's backing us.

 God, I will remember your rainbow when the future unnerves me.

Make a special effort during the next rainfall to find the right place from which to see the rainbow.

■ SPECIAL PLACES—NOW AND THEN

Matt. 25:34: "Take . . . the kingdom prepared for you . . . ."

Because of God's unique ability to compare what we now experience with what we soon will see, our loving Creator must be brimming with the anticipation of actually removing us to paradise.

Yet, while we live in our environment of flawed and inferior loveliness, he affirms our affection for this finite place. We call it "home" here and, because God knows us infinitely, God understands (even better than we do) what is meant by the term.

I find comfort in these thoughts when I face the fact that each one I love and that I myself must leave this world of oaken forests and purple mountains for a place unknown. I reflect on the observation by Alan Gussow in his *A Sense of Place* (Acclimatization Experiences Institute, 1983): "The catalyst that converts any physical location—any environment if you will—into a place, is the process of experiencing *deeply*" (p. 45). Because of his statement, I realize that the preciousness of my own backyard, of the woodlot where I pray, and of the familiar trails that pull my tensions from me has been developed by the experiences I have had there. Then, when I can imagine walking with Jesus and his saints through the splendors of a second Eden, a created place unmarred by sin, I suddenly feel comfortable with the notion that soon "I will be going home."

 God of nature, show me a special place where I can regularly meet with you.

Visit your "special place" for a time of prayer.

■ THE DARKER THE NIGHT

2 Cor. 12:9-10: "My grace is sufficient for you" (v. 9).

One night when my husband and I were in Canada, we walked down to the lake in front of our cottage. To my amazement, we saw the Big Dipper reflected in the water.

"I have never seen the stars so bright," I said.

"That's because you have never seen a night so dark," my husband replied.

Our experience there struck me as an illustration of God's grace which is always sufficient to supply our needs. The Bible assures us that when suffering and evil tip the scales, God is right there ready to pour out the extra measure of grace needed to put life into balance again. Just as starlight can be brightened by darkness, God's nearness can be accentuated by trials.

A statement in Catherine Jackson's paraphrase of Hannah Whitall Smith's classic, *The Christian's Secret of a Happy Life* (World Wide Publications, 1979) sums it up well: "If you side with God, you cannot fail to be victorious in every encounter. Whether the result is joy or sorrow, failure or success, death or life, you will be able to say, with Paul, 'But thanks be to God, who in Christ always leads us in triumph. . .' (2 Corinthians 2:14 RSV)" (p. 137).

So, even if you are surrounded by darkness now, look upward and expect to see God's light.

 O Jesus, bright and morning star, attend to my heartaches and those of my sisters and brothers in the faith.

Spend one evening this month studying the stars from a dark vantage point.

■ KNOWING EVERY STAR

Ps. 147:4-6: "He determines the number of the stars and calls them each by name" (v. 4).

Our sun is one of billions of stars in the galaxy. On clear, dark nights you can see a portion of our swirling galactic pinwheel. It's called the Milky Way, and it's composed of the blur of stars that we can see from our location on the galactic disk. Even as our earth is rotating around the sun, our sun is traveling around the mysterious center of the galaxy. At our "cruise" rate of 150 miles per second, one round trip takes 225 million years.

The speed of light is about 186,000 miles per second. It takes approximately eight minutes for light to reach us from the sun. It takes approximately four years for light to reach us from our next-nearest star. That makes our nearest star neighbor about four light-years away. Our entire galaxy, from edge to edge, is estimated to be 100,000 light-years wide.

Even more remarkable than this is the notion that beyond the reaches of our galaxy speed innumerable other galaxies spread out in the void of space.

The next time you go to prayer, remember that you are addressing the King who rules over all of that!

 Lord, with humility I ask to be kept close to you. O ruler of the universe, you are my God!

Take a trip to a planetarium to learn more about the universe.

◼ HEAVENLY LANDMARKS

Job 9:9-11: "He is the Maker of the Bear and Orion" (v. 9).

Job's specific naming of well-known constellations impresses on us that the stars are part of the natural setting in which God has revealed himself throughout the centuries of time. Like the Mount of Olives, the Sea of Galilee and other natural landmarks, the stars give us tangible reminders that Jesus lived on the earth just as we do.

It gives me joy to know that Job (and probably many other faithful believers from the past) looked up at the same stars I see and recognized in them the creativeness, beauty, and faithfulness of God. Some nights when I stand looking outward into space, I share another experience in common with my brother Job—that of sensing that the God who made the universe has silently passed by me, less than a breath away.

How great it is to share a heritage with the saints of old—to know the God who made everything and who loves us all!

 Lord, how very, very great you are!

Learn to use a simple star chart (available through museums, schools and supply houses) to identify seven of the most easily recognized constellations.

■ LIKE LIGHTNING

Matt. 24:27: "For as the lightning comes . . . so will be the coming of the Son of Man."

Severe electrical storms make an impression on us. The lightning that characterizes these events is similar in nature to a gigantic spark. Within the churning thunder clouds, powerful electrical charges build up. At the top, a cloud can carry a positive charge while at the bottom it can hold a negative one. When the air can no longer serve as an insulator, an electrical pathway forms between clouds or between clouds and land. Then we see a powerful current of electricity rapidly produce a flash.

The temperature within a lightning bolt may be hotter than the surface of the sun. Such tremendous heating sends such violent shock waves through the air that the sky explodes with a loud trembling thunderclap. The noise made by this rapidly moving air reverberates off hills and mountains.

No wonder lightning and thunder will attend Christ's return, for he will roll back the clouds forever and reclaim the earth from the grips of its enemies. Such transformation will be more powerful, more highly charged, more shock-producing than the sum of all the thunderstorms we have witnessed thus far.

Jesus, I thank you that the thunderstorm gives me a glimpse of what is to come.

Judge the closeness of a lightning stroke by counting the seconds between the flash and the crash. Then divide the number of seconds by five to determine the number of miles.

■ AN EAGLE'S TECHNIQUE

Isa. 40:28-31: "They will soar on wings like eagles" (v. 31).

Everything about a swift-flying bird supports its flight. Its bones are hollow and strengthened with light-weight inner struts. Its breast muscles are massive and organized in such a way that breathing is synchronized with the flapping of wings. Its feathers serve both to streamline the body and to catch the wind for flight. Each feather can be moved independently so that the bird can adjust to make maximum use of air currents.

Some birds fly fast and furiously. Eagles and hawks, in contrast, have long, broad wings that enable them to soar. By watching the birds of prey follow along their favorite migratory routes, you can learn much about their migratory techniques and perhaps something about your faith journey as well. Hawks and eagles can soar because of their great sensitivity to air movements and their physical abilities to take advantage of them.

Today the Holy Spirit wants to carry you along in the same way that a gentle updraft takes the eagle nearer to its home. Trust in God's unseen support. Stretch out your wings of faith and rest in the Lord.

  God, renew my strength!

Spend a day observing birds of prey in flight.

■ IN THE BAG

Matt. 13:3-23: "A farmer went out to sow his seed" (v. 3).

An Audubon Society member once distributed the canoe-shaped seed pods from his trumpet-creeper vine to others in his local chapter. He shared them so that the members could work together to create better habitat for hummingbirds. One of the women who received a pod that evening put it into her purse for safe keeping. She forgot about the seed pod until weeks later when she found it had "exploded" inside her pocketbook and spread its seeds into every crack and corner. The seeds were indeed "safe" at this point, but also totally unproductive.

Often we treat the Word of God like that woman treated her trumpet-creeper pod. We appoint ourselves to the responsibility of holding the gospel in "safe-keeping" and of sharing it only when we feel that someone might be responsive to it. We are silent about our faith with those who we deem "are satisfied with their secular life-style," or "are too scientific and logical to listen to what I have to say," etc. Our sort of spiritual "selective planting," however, may keep someone from hearing the good news of Christ. The parable reminds us that the responsibility for productivity should rest with the "soil" and not with the "sower." Let us ask God, then, for the wisdom and the boldness to share the good news with all our friends and acquaintances and not just with a selected few.

Jesus, make me gentle yet bold. Grant me the opportunity to talk about you with my friends.

Try introducing a common wildflower to your yard by broadcasting the seeds from dried pods.

■ LEANING ON OTHERS

2 Peter 1:3-9:   "His divine power has given us everything we need for life . . ." (v. 3).

Dodder is one of the most fascinating types of parasitic plants. It rambles over other weeds with so many twists and turns that it may appear to be a discarded clump of tangled orange yarn tossed carelessly to the side of the trail. As soon as dodder is established, its roots die off and it becomes dependent on others. Its white bell-like flowers take their cues from the chemicals of the plant from which it steals its nourishment. They bloom when flowers of the host plant do because they have assimilated the hormones of the parasitized plant.

Even though we sometimes like to think of ourselves as independent beings, we assimilate the characteristics of others quite readily. Research, for example, has shown that those who watch a great deal of television tend to perceive the real world as being similar to the "world" portrayed on TV. The views of our closest companions and the nature of our sources of relaxation and support definitely affect our spiritual lives. Consider your friends and pastimes. Are your relationships causing you to grow more like Christ? Or are you assimilating characteristics of those outside the faith and, like dodder, allowing your root system to wither away?

 Lord, help me to lean on you.

Study one parasitic plant growing in your area.

■ LIGHTED LAMPS

2 Sam. 22:29: "You are my lamp, O Lord. . . ."

Lightning bugs (sometimes called fireflies) are soft-winged beetles that set the midsummer fields a twinkle.

Each firefly employs bioluminescence to attract a potential mate. In most species, the males fly about while the females sit on or near the grass. The color and pattern of these blinking lights bring fireflies of the same species together.

In the laboratory, scientists are able to reproduce the cold, eerie light that the fireflies make. However, researchers still are uncertain about how the little creatures make the light appear and disappear at a fast twinkling pace. Even though it remains unexplained, no one can deny that this can be done by this familiar insect species. For this reason, the firefly can become an example of the unexplainable, yet undeniable, relationship that the believer has with God.

Some will say there is no God to depend on. Others will state that God does not associate with mortal beings. But by faith in the word of God and by experience, the believer has come to see that he or she is not merely flitting through a meaningless, dark existence called life. For the Christian, God is light. Even when we head into the darkness, God will be our light.

 Lord, I believe in you even when the darkness of doubts says that I should not.

Catch a firefly and let it light up the palm of your hand with its soft glow.

■ LESSONS FROM THE SEAS

James 1:6: ". . . he who doubts is like a wave of the sea. . ."

More than 70% of the earth's crust is covered by oceanic waters. In addition to holding perhaps 315 million cubic miles of water, the seas have contained a vast number of spiritual lessons for many different observers and authors. For nineteenth century poet Robert Montgomery the ocean was an "impassioned orator, with lips sublime" whose waves were "arguments to prove a God." For the English poet Byron, the oceans were a "glorious mirror, where the Almighty's form glasses itself in tempests." For the German statesman Karl Wilhelm Humboldt, the sea was "a great natural power" that "follows eternal laws which are imposed by a higher power."

Take a stroll along the shore sometime and see what the sea says to you. Does the constant movement of its waves speak to you of fluctuating philosophies or of the ever-present movement of God's Spirit? Does the oceans' depth—at their greatest plunge nearly seven miles down—remind you of sin being tossed into the sea and remembered no more or of God's even greater vastness than the ocean valleys that have been made? What lessons appear to be written in the numberless grains of sand at your feet? Write down your meditation so that you can reflect on it again even when you are landlocked and far away from the shore.

 Lord, let your restless, energetic waters speak to me of you.

Collect a shell or some other reminder of the sea. Display it someplace where it can remind you of the oceans' presence on Earth.

■ THE WONDER OF IT ALL

Psalm 8: "When I consider your heavens. . ." (v. 3).

As a writer and an avid reader, I like to carry along a volume of some author's works when I'm traveling through that person's home territory. I have read the words of Henry David Thoreau near Walden Pond and the diary entries of John Muir in the shade of Yosemite's trees. I appreciate the words more when I am surrounded by the environment that nurtured the ideas in the artist's mind.

I do the same thing with the holy Scriptures. I enjoy reading the Bible outdoors, surrounded by the things that God himself has made. In her book *The Sense of Wonder* (Harper and Row, 1956) Rachel Carson, the famous spokeswoman for ecological concerns, once wrote: "If I had influence with the good fairy who is supposed to preside over the christening of all children, I should ask that her gift to each child in the world be a sense of wonder so indestructible that it would last throughout life, as an unfailing antidote against the boredom and disenchantments of later years. . . ."

As a Christian I have come to believe that the best way to protect a child's inborn "sense of wonder" is to introduce him or her to the Author of the work. Better than the activity of "a good fairy" is our direct access to the vibrant Spirit of the Creator God.

 You, O Lord, are a master designer. I wonder at all you have made.

Do something to help another person come to a deeper appreciation of the natural world.

■ FAIR AS THE MOON

Song of Sol. 6:10: "Who is this that appears . . . fair as the moon . . .?"

The moon can steal the show in the nighttime sky even though it has no light of its own. Over the course of each lunar month we see different portions of its sunlit side from our place on earth.

The moon's dependence on the sun's light is even more dramatically represented during a lunar eclipse. This event occurs when the earth comes between the sun and a full moon. As the moon passes earth's shadow, it takes on a coppery glow.

Corrie Ten Boom saw the spiritual parallel of this natural event. She wrote in her book *Each New Day* (World Wide Publications, 1977) "We are moons. God is our sun. If the world comes between the moon and the sun, it is dark. The insecurity of the world is meant to be the raw material of our faith. Surrender to the enemy means death, but surrender to Jesus means life. Confess, commit, claim His presence." We are made "blameless and pure, children of God without fault in a crooked and depraved generation, in which you shine like stars in the universe" (Phil. 2:15).

As long as we stay in the light, we have hopes of being like Christ, who is "as fair as the moon."

 You, O Lord, are beautiful beyond description. Shed your pure light on us.

Make it a habit to observe the phases of the moon. Check into the date of the next lunar eclipse.

■ NO ORDINARY DAY

Ps. 118:24: "This is the day the Lord has made . . . ."

My favorite opening to a nature walk is to have each participant in my group find a "pretty stone." Since we often start our walks near a gravel parking lot, it is common for everyone to return with the same sort of stone. When each person has had time to study the pebble he or she has chosen, I gather all the pebbles in my hands. Then I spread them out for all to see, and I ask each participant to describe his or her stone to another in the group. Everyone in the group is amazed when the listeners can consistently retrieve from the collection the stone they have heard being described. Like many other professional naturalists, I use the exercise to show persons the importance of being observant.

But, at one point, God used this pebble-finding game to teach me a lesson all my own. My lesson superceded the truth that no rock, or leaf or seashell is exactly like another. With the pebbles, God impressed upon me the fact that no day is like another. My mental perception up to that point had been that workdays, Saturdays, and Sundays composed a routine cycle. My ungratefulness about each new day dulled my ability to anticipate God's workings in my life.

Now I see it is impossible to wake up to an ordinary day when the Author of Life is working out for me a constantly changing sequence of events. Now I see my responsibility to praise God for each new day.

 God, thank you for life!

Put seven stones in a box. Each day remove one as a reminder that this will be no ordinary day.

■ ROOM FOR CHRIST

Matt. 8:20: "Foxes have holes and birds of the air have nests."

Often at sunset you will see silhouettes of waterfowl winging their way home to some secluded section of lake or pond. You might just as easily see masses of noisy blackbirds vying for resting places in a grove of trees. If you watch, you might see squirrels tuck themselves into the holes of trees or chipmunks heading underground.

Even before night completely overtakes the land, nocturnal animals such as deer, raccoons and skunks leave their secure daytime abodes for a night of wandering. The systematic movements of animals at dawn and dusk bring to mind Jesus' words about himself. Even though God was the creator of all the animals, God did not come to earth to inhabit some splendid mountain castle, or forest mansion, or royal palace. Being God, Christ could have made himself a secure resting place anywhere he chose. Instead, he fulfilled his mission of being a resting place for others by drawing believers to himself. In truth, there is only one dwelling place that God desires, and that is the room in a human heart.

 "O Come to my heart, Lord Jesus; there is room in my heart for thee."

—Emily E. S. Elliot

Spend one evening this week watching how diurnal (day-active) animals prepare for night's return.

■ HANDMADE HOMES

John 2:12-23:   " 'Destroy this temple, and I will raise it again in three days' " (v. 19).

Building birdhouses can be a rewarding hobby. Before you start construction, study house plans from your local Audubon Society or another reliable source. Choose a design that coordinates the size of the opening with the type of bird you want to attract. Make sure the house has drainage holes and that it can be opened for seasonal housecleanings. Once the building phase is completed, put your birdhouse in a safe place that meets the habitat requirements of the birds you intend to serve. Then wait.

Soon rowdy house wrens will set your little structures swinging. Purple martins will twitter with satisfaction (and eat the mosquitoes in your yard for no extra charge) as they move into your multifamily highrise unit. Phoebes and robins will sit smug and silent as they incubate their eggs in nests on the platforms you have placed under the eaves.

Get involved with some group's effort to improve bird habitats. As you develop friendships within the group, look for the opportunity to share that Christ also is in need of a dwelling place in each person's heart.

 Lord, I pray that soon *(name a friend who is not a Christian)* will open the door of his/her heart to you.

Work on your "housing project" at least one day this month.

■ NO LONGER EDEN

Gen. 8:18—9:3: "Be fruitful and increase in number" (v. 9:1).

Many modern thinkers scoff at the idea that environmental problems are rooted in sin. Yet, acknowledging our intrinsic sin-nature opens the way for feasible explanations of our environmental crises. Right now, we are pitted against diminishing natural resources, a polluted closed life-support system, and bulging populations. While no one can say what earth would have been if sin had not been, some things are clear.

Apart from sin our world would not be suffering from the fallout of greed, selfish ambition and expedience. Apart from sin, we would still be relying on God's wisdom and judgments, instead of our own.

Unfortunately, some respected environmentalists have suggested that the start of our problems was the Judeo-Christian belief that God instructed humankind to be fruitful and to subdue the earth. As believers in the Word of God, we must be ready to state our view that our present situation is not the result of what God said but of how humankind responded to it.

More than that, we must be actively reconciling our own life-styles with our beliefs. Our faith calls us to be good stewards of the earth.

 Lord, how's my stewardship?

Read a book on simplifying your life-style and make at least one substantial modification in your living habits.

■ A NEEDED PROCLAMATION

Isa. 52:7: "How beautiful on the mountains are the feet of those who bring good news, who proclaim peace, who bring good tidings, who proclaim salvation, who say to Zion, 'Your God reigns!' "

For a variety of reasons, our best articulators on the subject of nature are pretty much mute concerning God. I often read their eloquent words with a sense of hollowness. Few of them probably would have subscribed to English poet Gerard Manley Hopkins' statement that, "The world is charged with the grandeur of God."

It also concerns me that our finest spokespersons for our faith often have failed to elucidate our thinking on the relationship of humankind and the natural world.

Whenever we come in contact with persons who are making the preservation of the physical world the center of their life's motivations, we have a responsibility to introduce them to the Creator of the world.

Likewise, when we meet persons who feel that Christians can pursue things eternal with no regard for the natural working of the world at hand, we need to remind them that God made an earthly home for us.

 Lord, my life is so marred by sin. Yet, let it be an example of reverence for you and for all your creation.

Familiarize yourself with one of America's nature writers. Try your hand at writing your own reflection of the interaction between humankind and the natural world.

■ A CALL FOR ACTION

Ps. 1:1-3:   "Blessed is the man who does not walk in the counsel of the wicked" (v. 1).

Because we see the earth as God's possession and not as our own, we Christians should be leading the way for simple living that does not consume more than its moderate share of resources.

Because we acknowledge that treasures in heaven are more important than possessions on earth, materialism should not be allowed to infiltrate the church.

Because we believe that we are created beings, made in the image of our God, we should see that living things have their own value because they have been created by God, even as we have been.

Because we believe that to have respect for God, for other human beings and for the world is in keeping with God's original intent for creation, we should have no involvement with any practice that compromises our reverence for life.

 Lord, my convictions may make the path ahead a difficult one. Even so, let me succeed in living a life that pleases you.

Read a book such as Francis A. Schaeffer's *Pollution and the Death of Man: The Christian View of Ecology* or Rachel Carson's *Silent Spring* to expand your understanding of the environmental crisis.

■ THE FINAL CHAPTER

Rev. 21:1: "Then I saw a new heaven and a new earth . . . ."

The variety of life on earth cannot be fully appreciated in the short life span of one observer. It would be too great a task to savor each plant and animal on earth, for there are many natural treasure chests, from desert to ocean, in which to look.

Even if we could exhaust the riches of this present earth, we still would not be caught up with God's creative energies. For, by God's grace, we will live to see the day when the Master Designer folds up the present worn tapestry of life and replaces it with a masterpiece that cannot be flawed.

What will God's new earth and heaven be like? We cannot say, but what we already know about Jesus Christ and about the natural world at present gives us cause for glorious expectations.

In her book *Each New Day* (World Wide Publications, 1977) Corrie Ten Boom wrote, "Think of stepping on shore and finding it heaven; taking hold of a hand and finding it God's; breathing new air and finding it celestial; feeling invigorated and finding it immortality." That, in the words of Corrie Ten Boom, is what lies ahead for us.

 Thank you, God, for the present heaven and earth and for the new ones that are to come.

Each day, consciously look for one "gem" in nature. Each day consciously remember that a new earth will come.

■ GOD'S MASTERPIECES

Ps. 24:1-2: "The earth is the Lord's, and everything in it, the world, and all who live in it" (v. 1).

The famous American naturalist John Muir traveled from Kentucky to Florida on foot soon after the close of the Civil War. Along the way, a robber stole his bundle. When the man discovered that it contained only items for personal hygiene, one change of underclothing, two books of poetry and a New Testament, he promptly returned it to Muir and went his way.

Though Muir traveled as a poor peasant, he had great wealth on his journeys because of his keen sense of observation and his appreciation for the multiplicity of wild plants.

Nature study can bring joy for a lifetime. It can be practiced anywhere. It can be done anytime. And, best of all, it can give us a constant, common bond with God.

For God said all that he made "is good." By having an interest in the natural world, we share with God an appreciation for life. What richer collection of masterpieces could be ours than those displayed in our own backyards by the Master Artist!

 "Praise God from whom all blessings flow; Praise him, all creatures here below; Praise him above, ye heavenly hosts; Praise Father, Son, and Holy Ghost. Amen."

Start a journal in which to record nature observations, scriptures, prayers and meditations throughout each season of the year.

■ A GLIMPSE OF GOD

Rom. 1:20-32: "For since the creation of the world God's invisible qualities—his eternal power and divine nature—have been clearly seen, being understood from what has been made, so that men are without excuse" (v. 20).

Theologians often link the development of religion with humankind's observations and interpretations of natural phenomena. Their theories should not surprise us, for the Romans passage tells us that the nature of the Creator is reflected in what has been made. We also know that in every age tremendous energy has gone into explaining the various workings of the natural world.

Learning more about any area of science can increase our appreciation for the complexity of nature. As Christians we must also allow such study to increase our awe for the God who brought it all into being.

If we do not, we may someday find ourselves akin to those who saw themselves wise in their own eyes and neither glorified God nor thanked him.

Combining nature study with Bible readings can be an exciting way to explore the earth. "This is what the Lord says: 'Heaven is my throne and the earth is my footstool'" (Isa. 66:1). Let the marvels of nature be to you a witness of the marvels of God.

 Thank you, Lord, for the earth you have made. Let me never take its wonders for granted.

Set aside at least one hour this week for nature study.

■ THE DARK BEFORE THE DAWN

Rom. 8:22-25: "But if we hope for what we do not yet have, we wait for it patiently" (v. 25).

The predawn world is a treat to your senses, even if it requires your getting out of a cozy bed to enjoy it. There's a certain silence, a unique penetrating dampness, a particular chill that comes only before sunrise.

Because of the convenience of artificial light and heat, we no longer await the morning with the same anticipation held by those who spend each night in the dark and cold. Yet, a predawn walk can stimulate our latent appreciation for dawn. On such a walk we might encounter a shy deer or a tired raccoon making its way to a hollow log to sleep the day away. In the dim light, birds and daytime animals begin to stir.

Your greatest joy after a damp, cold walk, however, may be in catching a glimpse of sunrise and in feeling the first warm rays of the sun. If so, let the moment emphasize to you a spiritual truth as well as a physical one. No one who hopes for dawn is ever disappointed. With the same certainty, those who look for God are sure to be rewarded—both now, by gaining a sense of his daily presence, and in the future, by sharing in his eternal glory.

 Great is your faithfulness, O God, both to the world and to me personally. Today, again, I put my trust in you.

Take a predawn hike by yourself or with others. Find a good location to enjoy the sunrise.

■ EACH NEW DAY

Gen. 1:1-5: ". . . and there was morning—the first day" (v. 5).

Who can comprehend the splendor of that first morning, of that precise moment when light broke through the all-encompassing darkness for the *first* time?

Likewise, who can comprehend the awesomeness of the God who accomplished the act by the utterance of his words?

Yet, each day of our own experience brings us face-to-face with both the creation and the Creator of that first day. Too often we allow fatigue and pressures of the coming day to take away the richness of the mornings we receive from God. This is not new to our generation. Even in Old Testament times it was said, "If a man loudly blesses his neighbor early in the morning, it will be taken as a curse" (Prov. 27:14).

Still, for those who rise and meet a dawn, there can be great rewards both in the natural beauty seen and in the worship time experienced by focusing on God at the start of a new day. Even if you're not a "morning person," rise early one day this week. Watch the sunrise in silence. Then praise God for another day.

 Lord, at the start of this new day I give you praise. May my use of it be pleasing in your sight.

Make a new commitment to thank God for each new day even before you get out of bed.

■ THIRSTING FOR GOD

Psalm 42: "Deep calls to deep in the roar of your waterfalls" (v. 7).

It is easy in our busy lives to push our intimate times with God to the fringe of our experience. How many times have you said, "I must find a few minutes today for devotions"?

Statements like this rise from our "head knowledge" that each day should be centered on God. Yet, especially when things are going well, we often let a mundane secularity crowd out our moment-by-moment expectant relationship with God.

If we are honest with ourselves, we admit the dryness of this style of living. Just as a thirsting deer knows that water will be its only satisfaction, so we as Christians know that our only recourse is to turn again to God. That "turning," which is repentance, can be difficult unless we willfully break away from our daily concerns for a time.

The world of nature provides a good setting for our coming back to God. At first the divine presence may seem only as sparsely refreshing as the dews that lay on Mount Hermon. As we wait, however, our souls are watered by spiritual streams, the culmination of God's washing away each confessed sin. Finally, like a deafening waterfall that totally drowns out all surrounding stimuli, our experience with God is awesome again and deep beyond description.

 God, wash over me with your forgiveness. Immerse me in your love. Refresh me with your presence as I turn again to you.

Sit by a waterfall and let its intensity be the setting for a time alone with God.

IMPERFECTIONS IN THE REFLECTIONS

2 Cor. 3:7-18: "And we, who with unveiled faces all reflect the Lord's glory, are being transformed into his likeness with ever-increasing glory . . ." (v. 18).

A lake surface can reflect the beauty of shoreline and sky only when it is still. Often a lake is mirrorlike only at dawn and dusk when the winds of the day are calm. Even then, an almost perfect reflection can be shattered in a moment by the splashdown of a pair of geese or the jump of a fish. Quiet waters may suddenly shimmer with the underwater movement of a snapping turtle or the surface hatching of a thousand-plus water insects. In nature, there is always a reason for the stirring of calm waters.

As Christians we are to reflect the glory of God with our lives. Yet, often there are stirrings within us that distort or destroy our ability to mirror God. "As water reflects a face, so a man's heart reflects a man," says Prov. 27:19.

Examine the reflection that your own life gives. Is the inner tranquility you need to reflect God's love marred by external distractions or internal cares? Are "winds" of doubt and discouragement rippling your faith?

Meditate on Christ's words: "Peace I leave with you; my peace I give to you" (John 14:27).

Jesus, I give you my worries and I claim your peace as my own.

Spend time by quiet waters. Study landscape reflections. Then find a natural mirror that shows a reflection of your own being.

■ THE MARK OF WISDOM

1 Kings 4:20-34: "(Solomon) described plant life, from the cedar of Lebanon to the hyssop that grows out of walls. He also taught about animals and birds, reptiles and fish" (v. 33).

It seems peculiar that the wisdom of Solomon, a king with tremendous financial and political powers, should be exemplified by his "nature lessons." Certainly, his knowledge of nature enriched his writings.

Yet, perhaps the Jewish historian shows us another aspect of Solomon's wisdom as well. The king must have been a keen observer who studied the life-style of each creature and plant. He observed not only those things of obvious importance (like the valuable cedars), but also those things of insignificance (like the hyssop in the walls).

Good observers are interested in the facts. They understand the significance of details and savor the variety inherent in each situation. Good powers of observation can lend themselves as foundations for good judgments, and good judgments are, in themselves, pillars for wisdom.

 Lord, thank you for the uniqueness of each day in my own experience. Give me wisdom to live each day according to your will.

Spend 10 minutes in a field or forest counting the number of different plants and small creatures that you see.

■ EACH ONE UNIQUE

Psalm 104:24: "How many are your works, O Lord!
In wisdom you made them all; the earth is full of
your creatures."

It is quite a task to be even an amateur ornithologist
(for there are more than 1700 species of North
American birds), or entomologist (for there are more
than 88,500 kinds of North American insects). Yet,
continual study will bring to you a knowledge of
animals common to your part of the country.

Each species that you learn to know will be different
from the rest. The biologist knows that no two types of
animals maintain exactly the same life-style. Therefore,
no two species are in direct competition with one
another. Each has its own space and its own function
in the natural world and in God's plan.

People are that way, too. Despite the many
hundreds of acquaintances that you might have, no
two persons have exactly the same role or place in
your life. Each person is a special gift from God.

Take time today to rejoice in the diversity that God
has put into life.

Lord, I thank you for _____ (list different
persons and mention what each one means to
you).

**Pick a specific area of nature study and get a field
guide on that topic.**